Widowed,

But Not Wounded

The Hustle & Flow

of 13 Resilient

Black Widowed

Women

Sabra Robinson

BookLocker.com, Inc. | Florida

2017

Layout by BookLocker.com, Inc.

Editing by Brian Thompson, Great Nation Publishing, Atlanta, GA

Nehemiah Publishing, Charlotte, NC

Cover Design by SelfPubBookCovers.com/AutumnSky

The Bible version used in this publication is King James Version

This one is for you, Herb.

To the contributing authors, thank you!

Sabra

"We are not meant to stay wounded.

We are supposed to move through our tragedies and challenges and to help each other move through the many painful episodes of our lives.

By remaining stuck in the power of our wounds, we block our own transformation.

We overlook the greater gifts inherent in our wounds — the strength to overcome them and the lessons that we are meant to receive through them.

Wounds are the means through which we enter the hearts of other people. They are meant to teach us to become compassionate and wise."

— *Caroline Myss*

(Reprinted with permission)

Contents

Foreword

This book unfolds amazing stories of grief, loss, and rediscovery; a process that you, the reader, will soon experience for yourself as you read through the pages ahead. We are living in a day that the experiences of others will help us along the journey of life, if we listen.

There are 13 stories told in this phenomenal book that will encourage and guide widows through one of the most challenging times. Sabra's vision hit the mark in developing a project by and for widows as a source of empowerment to aid widows in moving forward while combatting mental health, the church, self-care and many more issues faced while living a life without her husband. The purpose of this book is to provide stories of hope, empowerment, and healing for black women widows who are struggling to regain their life back after the loss of their husbands.

Sabra was a wife who was married for over twenty years with three offspring, two young men, and a teenaged girl. She and her husband married young while Sabra was still in college. She left the home of her parents to move in a home of her own to create her own family. Most of her young adulthood was spent being a mother and a wife; these loving roles dominate her life

To raise the family in a home of their own, Sabra and her husband found a home in the Charlotte, North Carolina area. Although a significant distance from her family cluster in Baltimore, Maryland as well as Mobile, Alabama, it was a location they embraced with love. They found a church home that spiritually nurtured them individually and collectively where both were active within the church family. For a period, life was filled with bliss. Then without warning, her husband was diagnosed with a terminal illness. Fortunately, Sabra was able to find employment while working from her home. After almost a year of home care, her husband passed away, leaving Sabra not only with grief from the loss of her husband but also the challenge of keeping her family together emotionally as well as financially.

As a widow, Sabra confronted many challenging issues that forced her to surface her inner strength. However, she knew that she had to regroup in many ways and on many levels. Although she had a family to help, they were at a great distance which made things difficult. Though many issues were tough, she found a way, and she was able to bring some normalcy to the family minus the loss of her husband.

Sabra did a monumental job keeping her family intact despite the financial and emotional turmoil while still addressing the grief of losing her spouse of twenty-three years. From what others perceived on the outside, Sabra had it all together as this superwoman. However, the truth was she was not a superwoman but a woman rarely showing the mental and emotional pain she endured because few people truly or fully understood her journey as a widow.

Sabra, with prayer, created a self-healing role as the founder of Black Women Widows Empowered to address the many issues she faced alone. In addition to writing her books, she created a blog and a Podcast radio program to allow women who are facing her similar issues to express, confront and help heal the challenges together. Sabra proudly takes the role as a Shepard (she is not a minister but is guided by her faith and personal relationship with God) to guide them to stay focus on the things that matter. She created a book with a collection of stories written by women about moving forward, healing and how they shifted their past to become a new now, which could be utilized as a toolbox or medicine cabinet of inspiration.

Remember, hope and healing are still possible even when the hustle seems unbearable, and your purpose and destiny have not been completed.

Dr. Stafford Sutton, Ph.D.

Chapter 1

The Hustle and Flow of Dr. Beverly Wallace: A Black Widow's Journey Toward Living Life Anew

"After he died, what really happened is she watched the days bundle into thousands, watching every act become the history of others, every bed more narrow... ." This portion of the poem by Lucille Clifton was read at my husband's memorial service. This piece of life-giving work published in "The Book of Light" gave me light and continues to do so on this journey called *life*. I didn't know this African American woman poet. Perhaps, if truth be told, I didn't know myself. Who I was and what I was supposed to do after my husband's death, I did not know. And I did not know that life would forever be changed after the hurricane.

No, my husband Richard had not died in a hurricane. He did die, however, two days after a hurricane, after Hurricane Katrina in 2005. I remember that season well, and I remember the various seasons of hurricanes and losses and new visions that occurred after my husband's death.

Twelve years have passed, and the turbulence of his death and life continue to teach me life lessons. I have come to realize that it's these interruptions in one's life plans, in the *"FLOW"* of life, that one begins to realize more of who they are. Reactions and responses to the death of one's husband are numerous. They change as with the seasons.

It is my hope that this piece will be shared with other women for their healing as they thrive as resilient black widows.

The Season of Death

Our colleague, Peter, stood up and read Lucille Clifton's poem. It was at the fourth service memorializing and celebrating Richard's life. Three prior services occurred in various parts of the country. But it was this one, in the chapel of the school in which Richard taught, that took me out. My brother walked me down the aisle when we processed for the service. Two days earlier

1

my brother argued with me as he perceived, that for Richard, I had not cried. I had cried, but it was in the quiet moments at night. It was when no one was around that I dealt with the loss of someone, who even after eleven years of marriage and now dead, I realized I did not fully know him. It was in that crowded chapel at the seminary where Richard taught, in a place full of Richard's students and colleagues, I finally shed my hidden tears in a very public way.

This service would be the last, almost a month after his death. My friend, Gwen, read the scripture. Richard's colleague from Pakistan, Charles, preached the sermon. Richard's, daughter, my stepdaughter, read a tribute to her father as if *she* was his true love and I wondered who I was.

I was no longer a wife. I was no longer a partner, not a faculty wife, nor a mother, (an identity I clung to but whose role had shifted because my children were now adults). I was no longer a stepmother as Richard's daughters proclaimed before the funeral; they had never wanted me to marry their father. I was not even a student (I had completed all of my coursework for my Ph.D. and was teaching in a new school in a new state). As I moved out of the house with real live bats (I do think it was a bat that scared Richard to death and caused him to have a heart attack at the age of 53), I was also moving out of a community that was questioning why I was not there when Richard died. I continued to question my identity. Who was I? What would be next for me in this season of my life?

A month prior I had moved to North Carolina and was pursuing my own hustle of teaching, and accepting a fellowship at a University in a state, which ten years later I would call home. I had been at the school less than a month when I got the call. I remember just before I went to my new office to try to call Richard once again, I had been in an auditorium with students making plans to respond to the Hurricane that tore through Louisiana and Mississippi. Before the hurricane, Richard and I had planned to meet in Atlanta to officiate his uncle's funeral. It was a week earlier that Uncle Kenneth had died. Three weeks prior, Richard's father had also died, and now I was to return to Minnesota because Richard had died, too. Not only did I have to prepare for his funeral and memorials, but I also had to prepare to live in the whirlwind of a new season I knew nothing of. I packed up the seminary-owned house in a month's time and returned to North Carolina to fulfill my commitment to teaching.

In North Carolina, I felt dead to myself. My daughter was not talking to me after feeling ashamed that I acted, "Brooklyn," on her when I yelled at Richard's first wife who entered our home to "protect" her daughters from me. My son, well, he was doing his own thing, and so here I was in a new city alone. There would be times when I returned from class and would immediately get into bed fully clothed. Who would care? Sleeping out of numbness, the aloneness unbearable, I was living and walking dead. And honestly, there were times when I simply wanted to end it all, even as I taught students in a class about dying and death.

I went to Brazil a month after Richard's death. Richard and I were to present a paper there. Peter, our friend, was there in Brazil as well. He took me out one evening to have a meal and to see the city. The darkness of the place, supposedly a vibrant one, was all a blur to me as was the year I spent trying to make my life anew. It was a friend, Gary, who would later be very present in my next season, who told me to get up and do something for someone else. And so, I did. Nine months later, at the end of the school year, I left North Carolina and went to face the residuals of the storm called death (or was it life?). Even though I was offered a permeant job of teaching, I decided to leave.

My journey took me to Mississippi. My bishop called and asked if I would go. I had lived and worked on the Gulf Coast before, so it was familiar. My new hustle was to work with those victims and families and churches who had experienced loss due to Hurricane Katrina. For almost two years my new hustle was to comfort and care for victims who lost so much. I buried myself in that work, but there were lessons for me to learn such as not taking the time to face my loss, confront my fears and not living my truth. It was in the season of Richard's death, risking leaving something, a job, that was certain, shifting the flow of my hustle that new learnings would also occur. I was encouraged to go to someplace familiar for a season for healing. I began to learn more about myself.

I went to grief counseling during this season. I had to take a good look at my marital relationship. I told my therapist that I married Richard because he was safe. But I really married out of fear; fear of being fully responsible for myself. I did want things to work out. Neither one of us had done the work of embracing who we were. Healing is a process I learned. It would take time. Unfortunately, because of the untimely death of my husband, his time ran out. I felt sad for him. But my time was not over. I had to come face to face with

3

me. There would have to be another season to go through before I would begin to understand this and do so. Another storm would occur. Another season of more intentional learning; a time I call, *The Season of an Illusion.*

The Season of an Illusion

He encouraged me to help someone else. He, however, did not tell me to help myself. He was an addiction, an excitement, and a fun person; he had been a constant ebb and flow of my life for almost thirty years.

Gary and I met when I was ending my first marriage. I was a walking zombie at that time and was even more afraid of living. I was afraid to speak up. I was afraid to take chances. I married my first husband because at the time it was the thing to do. But I was not happy. I did not have a voice. When I spoke, I was often silenced and discounted. It was not, however, how I wanted things to be, and I felt there was more to life. Gary entered my life. He was a married man at the time, but oh so charming, was he.

He bought me my first bouquet of flowers leaving them on my doorsteps. No man had ever done that for me. He took me dancing. No man had ever done that with me, and I was mesmerized by his charisma. But he was charming to other women as well. I thought that I was going to be the one who would settle with forgetting the words that he told me when I talked to him about my marriage – "don't settle".

Realizing that Gary was not one to settle down, I married Richard. It was safe. But the desire to live with abandonment was my passion. Then Richard died, and my relationship with Gary rekindled.

When I moved to Atlanta after my time in Mississippi, Gary was to move to Atlanta too. We were finally going to be together – so I thought. The addiction that he struggled with, however, took him in another direction. He entered rehab in another state, and I began my work of dealing with my own disease of co-dependency. Gary got better, but the illusion of 'happily ever after' would not be. My cards came crashing down when he told me he was to marry someone else.

"Watching every act become the history of others, every bed more narrow..."

The Clifton poem was telling my story. Yes, the bed became more narrow. The one who I had been in love with for more than thirty years, the one who I had hoped to marry and spend the rest of my life with, had decided that another woman of a lighter hue would become his wife. And I was left to grieve yet again.

I was to grieve the fact that I had loved someone who could not commit to a relationship with me. I grieved the illusion. But this was a different kind of grief; a different kind of loss because the person who I was grieving was yet still alive. My former professor, Pauline Boss, coined the term "Ambiguous Loss," and for sure this fits the description. I would see Gary at conferences and hear about him through colleagues. He was present, but the relationship was not. It was a different kind of grief because he was the one with whom I felt I could truly just be myself. I grieved the loss of intimacy, and I felt the hole in my soul that was getting bigger and bigger.

I watched from afar and wondered if my joy would return. I hoped that he was happy but was also angry and felt that he let my other sisters and me down. Why did he love a white woman? What was wrong with us? Or to be truly honest once again, the questions were: What was wrong with me? Was I too demanding? Was I too much of a bulldog, as another male friend who rejected me once said? Was my body not a sight of pleasure? Was I simply too old? Would my bed always be a bed for me alone? But I was simply in a season of an illusion of what living fully could be. My co-dependence did not serve me well. Healing and wholeness were not yet realized because my life was based on what I wanted it to be and not what it was. And then the season changed again.

The Season of a Possibility

Ten years after my husband passed, a new season was upon me. This next season occurred so unexpectedly. *The Season of the Illusion* took a toll on me. I did not know, however, that there would be another season - *The Season of a Possibility.*

I was not actively looking for this new season. I was resolved to the idea that my time had passed. I didn't realize a new season was in the making. I also did not know that in the flow of my life, this would be a short-lived season. I surely did not know that even in this *Season of a Possibility,* I would experience even yet again the loss of another man who I dearly loved.

I met Nate when I was working on a project for my mother. He, in turn, was helping in the community. Nate was assisting seniors in getting ramps built for their homes. Nate had come to my mother's house to check it out, and I met him at the back door. I remember I had crumbs on my lips (perhaps symbolic in that I had settled into accepting the crumbs of life). He helped me identify the crumbs and suggested that I wipe them away.

Nate was working on another project and asked me for my help. We were to be partners in a venture in teaching others how to care for themselves holistically. The magazine which he felt was his life work was to be called Revelation, and he wanted it completed before his 60th birthday.

We began to talk with each other on a regular basis. Not only did I share my current journey with him – the death of my brother, the illness of my mother, and the disillusionment with Gary, but he began to share his life journey with me as well. On one of our outings for coffee, he asked that I promise not to leave him as he struggled with the ebb and flow of his own life situation. I told him I would not.

Nate would engage his work as an engineer as I engaged in mine and would call me just about every morning to say hello and to check on mom and me. My work would often take me out of town as he traveled across the state of North Carolina.

In June of this year, I had just returned from a business meeting for the second time in a month. (my hustle of teaching takes me away from time to time.) Two weeks before my return from the first trip I had not heard from Nate for a couple of days. When we did talk, I told him he could not disappear on me like that again. I told him I would tell him my reason when we talked in person.

I did not want to tell him that not hearing from him reminded me of the death of Richard, my husband. I did not want to tell him that it was two days after Richard's death when his body had been found in our home that I would be told that my husband had died. I did not tell Nate after his 60th birthday celebration, just four months prior when he was hospitalized with congestive heart failure, that the occurrence frightened me. I did not tell Nate that I did not want him to disappear on me.

Nate and I did not have that conversation about my fears, but he promised me though that he would not do that again. Even now, I am writing this piece in a place where we first shared coffee, and I remember him telling me, "don't disappear on me." I, too, was going to hold him to this promise. Two weeks later I took another business trip. Upon my return, I again had not heard from Nate.

Well, Nate had died. Apparently, no one was able to reach me.

The day I found out that Nate had died I was obligated to care for another. I was to engage in a grief counseling session in my new practice (my new hustle) with a woman who a year prior had lost her own husband. That morning after I confirmed the news of Nate's death, I stood in the shower and cried like I never cried before. Perhaps it was all the many losses that I had experienced in the past twelve years. Perhaps it was the realization that I did not get a chance to say goodbye once again. I cried over the loss of my friend who seemed to have disappeared on me. And I cried for me and all the dreams of the possibility of life anew. Whether the dreams would have been actualized, the mere possibility was now gone with Nate's death.

That evening, I decided to care for myself and grieve. I rented a hotel room to be alone. Wondering if indeed I was like a Black Widow spider, I questioned: "Do all the men I love die because of me?" You see, when I was in college in my freshman year, a young man who liked me but I was afraid to engage him, drowned and died during our summer break. Richard, my husband, died of a heart attack; Andre', the one who said I acted like a bulldog died of colon cancer; Gary, well his love died and then there was now Nate. Was I in fact destined to have the death of the men I love to be a part of my life journey? Being with me, is that why they died?

In some African traditions, it is believed that a widow causes their husband's death. The death of a husband before his wife is viewed as unnatural and presumed that the wife might have had a hand in his death. She is treated inhumanely in some parts of Africa with Widowhood Rites imposed inclusive of exclusion and confinement, poor dressing, compulsory prayers and more, all because it is believed the widow has the power to cause death.

I laugh as I think of this as I don't have that kind of power. (Laughing at this thought would have been something that Nate would have done too, which was Nate's way of being in the world as well as his take on life.) But during one's grief experiences, one thinks of all sorts of crazy things. One thinks they can master control of the calamity caused by the hurricanes and storms that come with living. Nate taught me in his living that one could not. You go with the flow. Life is to be lived.

Nate entered my life. His presence would change my outlook on life. Our intimacy was so powerful even though we had not even kissed. This *Season of Possibility* would be a rich experience that would have me looking at who I was and how I lived and how I loved.

After the night of my lament when I took the time to talk with the spirit of Nate and to cry for the loss of his physical presence and his early morning phone calls, after grieving over the loss of a life of possibilities, I got up. I made plans to say my goodbye to Nate. I attended the funeral and watched as they wheeled his lifeless body out of the church. My body quivered with pent-up emotions. I thought I was about to fall. But as his body laid strong in his death, my body too got strong in the recognition I could stand and be okay. Nate was not going to disappear on me. His spirit would forever be with me. It is in my memories of Nate, of loving and living every day, not being afraid of dying, (we talked about his death two weeks prior to him dying), the willingness to live and love fully (a covenant that Nate made to himself and me after his 60th birthday and health scare) that I can be alright. I did not go to the cemetery but left and returned home to prepare for a trip to New York. And I vowed as Nate vowed, to live.

The Season of Life Anew

"Inseparable." The song began to play on the radio. The lyrics of the song gave me peace as I drove and thought about Nate. I now smile when I hear that song, and I play it repeatedly to be reminded of his presence. I promised not to disappear on Nate, and I do feel he kept his word too. Nate is with me.

With my husband Richard, his presence continues to guide me, too. Remembering them both remind me to love and love intentionally. Their spirit reminds me not to be afraid and to live and live with integrity. Even in the *Season of Illusion,* with Gary, while he is still alive, that relationship taught me the lesson of owning the desire to be known, fully known, to be fully naked and honest with others, but more importantly, naked and honest with myself.

Lessons from death have taught me well. Life's lessons have taught me too, and I am grateful for these experiences. So, what have I learned? To tell the truth is risky but also necessary for one's growth. To tell the truth about oneself and to oneself is even more crucial. I planned and lived my life based on the life of another - my husband, my lover, my friend. That strategy did not work. I know more fully now that I am responsible for living my life. Another lesson that I learned is that there will be a time when out of a desire to be loved, we embrace an illusion. Life is too short to live in make-believe. Years go by so quickly, and long life itself is not promised.

Life's seasons teach one to breathe even when winds of death attempt to, and often, wreak havoc. One learns that seasons constantly changes. But after each death, there is a resurrection. A widow decides to die or live in each new season. It is an ongoing process of deciding if one wants to be whole. As in the words of the writer, Toni Cade Bambara, when she raises the question in her work, *The Salt Eaters,* "so you sure sweetheart, that you want to be well. Just so you're sure sweetheart, and want to be healed, cause wholeness is no trifling matter. A lot of weight when you're well."

So… I will visit Paris this coming Springtime and Brazil anew this coming summer. A few trips I do remember: a trip to Italy three years prior; parasailing over the Gulf of Mexico when I cannot even swim; zip lining over the trees of Utah when I was sorely afraid of heights; a visit to Switzerland and Ghana; taking a cruise and dancing on St. Maarten's beach, (now devastated because of the more recent Hurricane Irma). I'm rebuilding my life while living without fear. A Resilient Black Widow she becomes. "Widowed" but not devastated by her wounds. As in the words of Lucille Clifton's poem, deciding and determined to do so, I LIVE.

Chapter 2

The Hustle and Flow of Danielle James: The Life of the 'Paparazzi' Party

The Beginning Before the Hustle and Flow

I was 32 years old when my husband died in a car accident June 2, 2013. The man I began dating at the age of 18, the man I lived with for ten years and was married to for five years; who I had two children with was gone in a blink of an eye. How was I going to go on? Who was going to help me raise our children? Why me? Those were the questions that kept going through my mind as I sat anxiously in the waiting room of Shands Hospital in Jacksonville, Florida, waiting for an update on my husband's condition.

On June 1, 2013, my husband, Marcus, prepared for work at 5 a.m. and, as always, he leaned over while I was still in bed and kissed my forehead. We were all packed and ready to travel 400 miles after he got off work to see his nephew graduate from high school the following Monday. One of his sisters and her son traveled along with our eight-year-old son, 2-year-old daughter, my husband and myself. We were in no rush to get there, so we made a few stops along the way. We had finally made it to Jacksonville, so I called my mom to let her know we made it safely; little did I know 15 minutes later my nightmare would begin. At that time, we did not have GPS on our phone, and he did not activate the ONSTAR in his Yukon Denali, so we were using MapQuest. While getting off to what he thought was the exit to his sister's house, he looked at the paper and realized it was the next exit. Upon veering back on the interstate, we were hit by a van. The SUV spun around hitting the rails having us facing ongoing traffic. When the truck finally stopped, I jumped out, not thinking or caring that I could have been hit. All I know is that my husband was bleeding from his mouth, nose, and ears! I was screaming and crying for help. A lady stopped and identified herself as a nurse and immediately began doing compressions on him. I thank God for her because had she not stopped, my children would have watched their father die in that truck.

The ambulance finally arrived. They began to check everyone. I was upset because all I wanted was for them to get my husband to the hospital. We were all walking and talking while my husband was in that driver's seat fighting for his life! As they used the Jaws of Life to get him out, I stood there crying, praying, begging God not to take him from us. Once they put him in the ambulance, I attempted to get in, but they refused to let me ride. His sister had made it to the scene by then so we followed the ambulance. We arrived at the hospital. I then attempted to go to the back, thinking if he saw me or heard my voice he would know his family was okay, and he would fight to stay alive; I was not allowed to go to the back.

I sat in the waiting room with his family until the doctor came in to tell me what I already knew, my husband was dead. I knew this because of the sickness that came over me while I waited. I closed my eyes remembering what happened just two hours ago. I saw him so clearly gripping the steering wheel so tight that his veins started popping out of his arms and hands. I knew he was gone because I could hear him asking God to take him and not his family. I sat there blaming myself. If only I had read the directions correctly. If only I could have told him to get off on Exit A rather than B, it would have been avoided.

Now what? How do I go to my sister-in-law's house and tell our children their father is dead? My family came as soon as they could. They tried to get me to go home, but I was not leaving until my husband's body was returned home. A couple of days later, I was finally back, but I could not go back to that place I called home, so I stayed with my mom for almost a month.

The pain I felt as a wife that had lost her partner-in-crime was extraordinarily heavy. I honestly thought it would last forever, but apparently, God had other plans for me. After the loss of my husband, my world came crashing down. I felt helpless, and no longer understood my purpose for living. All I could focus on and pray for was to get that precious moment back with the love of my life. I would have given anything for just one more hug, one more kiss, and the chance to say and hear I love you just once more time.

As a mother, I had to hide my grief because my children, especially my daughter, could feel my energy. She cried for her daddy every night for weeks once we went back home. I was going crazy inside due to the inability to stop her pain. He was the only man she'd ever loved. My heart aches for her as she only shared two precious years with him. My son developed anger issues, and I could see the death of his best friend was taking a toll on him. Our life was in shambles, and there wasn't a single thing I could do about it. I have endured a lot of heartache and pain during this time. My soul was lost, and I could not imagine my life without Mark.

One day, without reason, I took a long look in the mirror. I did not recognize the woman staring back at me. It was then that I realized it was time for me to pick up the broken pieces of my heart and began living again. I gained that "hustle-and-flow" mindset, and found a new motivation and drive to focus not only on myself but on two people who meant the world to me: my children.

Understand, it was not an easy process to undergo as I let PTSD and depression consume me. I went back to work a month after my husband's funeral and only stayed for 30 days. I was a case manager for nine years at a mental health facility. One of my job requirements was to transport consumers to and from their doctor's appointments. One particular day, I had an anxiety attack and thought someone hit us. It caused a reaction to my consumer, and then I knew I would not be able to work a job that required an abundant amount of driving. Now what? I am unemployed with nothing to do. I grieved for a full year in nothing but silence. During the day while the kids were in school, I would drink a bottle of wine, watch those four walls cave and incase me in agony, then proceed to lose my mind. I would kick, scream and punch walls. I was at the anger stage of grief. I cursed Mark out for leaving us daily. I asked God how could he take the only man who loved me; the man I spent my entire adult life with away from me.

As time went on, I focused on one day at a time and began picking up those broken pieces once again, but this time with more determination, sassiness, and gracefulness I lost along the way. I refused to allow my tragedy to keep me in bondage. I had to set myself free. I had to reclaim that strength and "hustle-and-flow" I prayed for, and I am now an entrepreneur that owns her own business and brands herself as "That Jewelry Lady." Yes, I am all that and more.

The Dating Hustle

The confidence of being an independent jewelry consultant allowed me to put myself back in the world of dating. I laugh at that statement because I did not know what it was like to date. Yes, my husband and I went on dates, but dating is conversing with multiple people to get to know them. I was not good in that area due to me loving fast and hard. My first encounter with dating took me by surprise because it was someone from high school who was a year older than me. I entertained the fact we could date. It had been 22 months since another man had touched me, and I was starting to feel the need of a man's touch. I figured since he would be moving out of town in three months we could just have fun. Well, it's all fun and games until you have sex and fall in love! Yes, I fell in love with the first man I slept with after my husband's death. I knew this dating thing would not work out for me because I could not show interest for more than one guy at a time.

I was not used to dating!

As I said, I began "dating" my husband when I was 18 years old. A year and a half later we were living together. I knew this man was leaving, yet I was pissed because of the feelings I felt for him. We tried the long-distance relationship, but of course, it did not work. I was hurt but still tried to move on. I came across another friend from a job I worked at when I was 17. This man knew my story, knew my pain and was very blunt with me. He said he could be a distraction and make me feel good with no strings attached. No kissing, no cuddling, just a distraction when I needed it. I thought that if I ran into him first, I probably would not have gotten my heart broken four months ago.

As time passed, I continue to work my business and building my team with major setbacks along the way; but it didn't stop my "hustle-and-flow." The next year, another old friend crossed paths with me, and it was an instant connection. A connection so deep I just knew this would be the end to this dating saga. I told him up front all of my flaws. I told him I was an emotional roller coaster who suffered from PTSD and depression. I told him I was clingy and craved attention. Well, of course, he claimed to understand, and we started a relationship. But this was not like the first relationship; we were going out on dates, staying the night with one another and he was cooking for me and buying me gifts! This was it; he was the one, so I thought. Well, again I fell in love too fast. The man who I told all of my flaws to finally admitted he could not handle them anymore. He said it most modestly, "you are too good for me." I wanted to slap him, wait, I think I did slap him. How dare he have me fall in love with him and soon decides I'm too good for him. This one hurt deeply. Here it is everyone that I love, I lose.

What in the hell is wrong with me?

My mind was thinking that I needed to date someone I didn't know. Two months after the break-up I met someone via Facebook. We hit it off and began dating. This guy and I dated long enough for him to meet my kids and this was a huge step for me. My son has finally accepted the fact that I was moving forward with my life. I no longer have to wait until my kids fall asleep and sit in my driveway talking like a teenager. This man can sit at my kitchen table, and we can converse like adults. But the tables had turned on me. Now I'm on the opposite end of insecurity. Not only was this man insecure but he was way too selfish. I put more into the relationship than he did and I had to step back and reevaluate my worth. This time I was the one doing the breaking up. Now it's time for me to stop trying to find someone to love me and put that same amount of passion in my business as well as myself.

A Paparazzi's Hustle

During that year of breakups, I began working as a payee representative for a non-profit homeless service center. Helping people is my passion. I was with that company for only a year and a half due to lack of funding. So here I am single, without a job but oh so happy! Now I focus on putting 110% in my Paparazzi jewelry business. My hustle and flow with my business have allowed me to build a team of more than 50 women who are seeking financial freedom. As Paparazzi consultants we feel that five-dollar jewelry may not change the world, but those who wear it will. I am proud of the woman that I have become. I am now a Premier Director, Crown Club 10 Member, and a member of the Life of the Party Bronze Access Program. I am no longer letting loneliness drive me into arms of men who are intimidated by my level of independence and success. My hustle and flow now come with strength, courage, and determination.

My Flow Endures

As an African American female, my strength comes from my Lord and Savior. I will forever devote my time as a devoted member of my church. This journey has taught me about myself and my spiritual relationship with God. He has been by my side each time, allowing me through my losses, my hurt, and my pain. I truly believe He has so much more for me to give to this world; at a time when I could not see that He was preparing me for a love I thought I would never find again.

I want to reassure anyone who has loved and lost, that this is not the end of your story, it is just the beginning of a new chapter. I pray that my story will inspire anyone that is seeking God, not just widows, but anyone who has felt pain, hurt or just confused about who you are. We are all connected by the loss and the pain we have endured.

When you see a widow, please do not pity her or label her with an unfortunate title. We do not want to be defined as a widow but as a survivor. I'm finally free.

Chapter 3

The Hustle and Flow of LaTisha Bowie:
Caterpillar, Cocoon, Butterfly, Evolution

Persecution is only effective to the degree you need acceptance from those talking about you. ~IV Hilliard

About a year ago I participated in a vision board activity facilitated by a sister at my former church. For the activity, we had to pick a card from a group of cards that were set on a table. We were to flip the card over to reveal a word written on the other side. Whatever word was revealed, we would use to create a vision board that represented who we were with a word that was opposite of what was on the card. I can't remember until this day the word that I randomly picked from the table. I can tell you however that I struggled heavily with it initially and did not want to complete the activity. During the activity, as I sifted through the magazines for pictures that represented me, I found a picture of a young lady that was very colorful. Her hair was beautiful, and there was a makeup brush floating over her. The young lady, however, had no face; where her face should have been was completely blank despite the beauty of her hair and facial structure. The picture was an ad for a major cosmetic line; the intent was to sell their makeup and brushes with the promise that their line would create beauty. But that's not what I saw when my eyes fell upon that picture. The picture resonated with me not because I saw a woman ready to create her beauty with makeup, but the blank face represented a woman with no identity. The woman with no face represented me.

I lost my identity somewhere along the way during my marriage, or maybe I had never developed an identity at all at the time that I entered my marriage. I came from an abusive home environment which ultimately culminated in me spending a significant amount of years in foster care. During those years I moved around a lot. I lived in a total of five foster homes and changed schools often. I had developed minimal relationships and had limited contact with my biological family. My husband became my connection to everything and everyone. Everything was connected to him—his family, his church, his friends, the people he grew up with. He was the church boy, and I was the street girl. I wanted to be accepted into his world, but that would prove to be difficult if not almost an impossible task.

We met at the church where he grew up. I was a new member, and admittedly a little rough around the edges. Few of the members actually talked me. In their eyes, I was the "burgundy blue haired girl, " and many of the parents cautioned their kids to "stay away from that street girl." I used to rejection, having experienced it most of my life from being bullied in school, to being rejected by my parents, foster parents, foster siblings, and my biological family. The one place that I thought I would finally find acceptance ended up being the place where rejection scarred me the most...the church. But I kept coming, and one day my late husband sat next to me and started a conversation. I instantly liked him. Initially, he accepted me as I was, not giving a care in the world concerning what other people said or thought about me. In our earlier years, he saw beyond the foster kid with the rough exterior and accepted me for who I was. I was his "Ruth" (the unchurched girl), and he was my "Mahlon" (church boy, Ruth's first husband before Boaz. Mahlon literally can be translated as "church boy"). From there we were together for 17 years until the morning of March 18th, 2011 when my husband, a licensed minister of the church, my Mahlon, put a gun to his head and took his own life.

Sometimes I feel as if I don't have a right to grieve as other widows. I wish I could say that those 17 years were glorious and wonderful. I wish I could say that I have the nostalgic feelings and memories that other widows have. Unfortunately, that's not my story. As the years progressed, my husband became physically, verbally, and emotionally abusive. During those years, I was not sure if this was due to his own mental health issues, the fact that his family really did not accept me, or that in his eyes, "the church" never really accepted him or treated him like he was good enough. He always strived to prove that he was not a "black sheep". The rejection of me by others consistently solidified those feelings of rejection within him. Approval and acceptance are what he strived for although he presented a confident persona to the public. Every pursuit and accomplishment in his life was a continuous effort to prove that he was worthy. I guess we were two peas in a pod because eventually, I did the same. Six years later, I now understand that it was a combination of all those elements that intertwined to create the perfect storm of insecurity within him that he, in turn, projected onto me.

I strived to please my husband, to transform from the rough around the edges foster kid to someone that he, his family, and the church deemed as acceptable. I made my best effort to fit into his world, but nothing I did was ever good enough. My efforts to support him in everything he endeavored to do, be a good wife/minister's wife, keep myself insignificant and in the background to be sure I never overshadowed him, to reach the unattainable bar that he set for me were all in vain. Was I a perfect wife? Woman? Human being? No way. But I tried. I wasn't allowed to exhibit anything but perfection or else I would be judged as unfit by all who surrounded us. If I expressed my displeasure in something I "always had an attitude," and if I reacted to a situation assertively I was labeled as "crazy". The criticism from all parties was consistent and relentless. I changed so much trying to gain the approval of others that one day I found myself standing in front of the mirror not able to match clothes for work and having no idea of how to comb my hair. The reflection staring back at me was blank. I was literally a walking nervous breakdown.

No matter how much God began to refine me, no matter how many degrees I began to obtain and how many licenses and positions I held in the church, I still did not gain his, nor the individuals around us approval or acceptance. I would always be that "burgundy, blue-haired" foster kid that walked into the church years before. Strangely enough, also as God began to refine me, much of the sentiment changed from "who are you?" to "who do you think you are?" As I began to increase my spiritual and secular education, the perception of those around us was now, "she thinks she's better than us, and she thinks she's better than you." This made things go from bad to catastrophic in my household.

As a minister myself, I have a very out-front gift, but I made efforts to make myself invisible and behind the scenes as much as possible so not give the impression that I thought more highly of myself that I should; or that I was trying to outshine anyone, especially my husband. I became a people pleaser. I rarely said *no* when asked to do something; I was 100% faithful and loyal in every area of my life to the detriment of my own health and personal tasks that I needed to accomplish for myself. I had become the ultimate "Yes" woman; I agreed to everything and questioned nothing. I rarely disagreed or stated my personal preference or opinion on a subject; if you liked it, I loved it. To be completely honest, I liken it to living my life as a chameleon, whoever you needed me to be, that's who I was so as long as you didn't reject me. Slowly, many people began to accept me, but of course, I rarely gave them any problems and was always there when they needed me. I always did what I was told and always agreed with the status quo. This reinforced my efforts to be a "good little saint" constantly. This conditioning taught me that if I were a "good girl" who did not buck the system, I would always be accepted.

My husband's death did not immediately free me from this mental conditioning, but rather for a time reinforced it. You see, when someone dies due to suicide there is typically blaming, guilting, and shaming directed at the family that is left behind. Especially the spouse. Couple that with the fact that my husband was a minister and you add an entirely new level of dynamics to the situation. Many people blamed me openly and secretly. Once again, I set out to be the "good girl" and "Super Christian" to prove his death was not my fault, that I was strong, that I was indeed a "Woman of God" and the person everyone had grown to love.

When death occurs, those of us raised in the church often develop this "Super Saint" Syndrome. Everyone around me told me that I was ok because I was a strong woman of God, a woman of prayer, a woman versed in the Word. They encouraged me to move forward and "get over it" because I had God on my side. So once again I put on the mask and masqueraded an identity that was not my own. Yes, I was a woman of God, but I was not strong at the time. I was broken, and my spirit was crushed. I kept up that charade for about a year until the grief caught up with me and I finally broke down and had a "Come to Jesus meeting" with God. No more pretending. I let Him know that I was angry, devastated, confused, questioned whether He was real, and flat out let Him know that I did not understand the situation I was in. He then helped me to realize that I was very hard on myself and that I was allowing people to rush my children and me through the grieving process for the benefit of their comfort.

Healing starts with acknowledging the fact that there is pain that needs to be addressed. Being a Christian or religious woman does not mean you are made of Teflon when death or tragedy knocks at your door. You will find that "getting over it" is an unreasonable expectation, but healing and wholeness are still attainable. Each year will always have its heavy and light moments, and you must align yourself with a network of people that will allow you to feel what you feel and help through those moments. Allowing myself to take off the mask and be transparent gave me the courage to begin the process of becoming who I was meant to be. What I also found when I removed the mask was the fact that our transparency frees others, no matter what positions we hold.

The very act of admitting to God that I was weak and broken, and then submitting to Him my broken pieces was the catalyst that began my evolution – my hustle. Who better to put the broken pieces of my life back together than the Potter Himself. When something is broken in its current state, it rarely can be repaired exactly like it was before. But that was ok. The *me* that I was before, was formed and molded by the hands of human opinion, by the need for approval and acceptance, by fear of rejection, and the need to please people. The need to prove I was worthy, that I was good enough to people that were always determined to make me feel inferior was no longer in existence.

God began to take those broken pieces and put them through fire to make them moldable again. See, when something is put through fire, it can be melted down and reshaped. I began to allow God to shape me into the person He intended for me to be. The process was/is not always pretty, comfortable, and most times painful; but standing with my true authentic identity intact is worth every minute on the Potter's wheel and every moment in the refining furnace. Does that mean I'm perfect and everyone likes me? Nope! But that's the beauty of it. I am not perfect, and I don't have to walk a perfectionist's path trying to please everyone. I no longer need acceptance from people unwilling to accept me. Of course, I have a need to belong...everyone does. But I now find my belonging among a network of friends who do not make me perform or fight for a place in their lives. Good, bad, ugly, or indifferent they accept me as I am, and do not abandon me in an attempt to manipulate me into being the person they prefer for me to be.

During the process of self-discovery, many significant people made an exodus out of my life. Some, not all, no longer wanted to be in a relationship with me because the person that I was becoming no longer benefit them. Ultimately, they wanted me to be the person I was when I was married to my husband. They wanted the *yes* person, the person that rarely spoke up for herself, the person that tried to avoid conflict, the person that made herself insignificant to be sure to not overshadow others, the person that wanted to remain invisible, the person that downplayed her accomplishments, and the person who agreed to everything and questioned nothing because I wanted so bad to be accepted. Some just didn't understand me; they were familiar and more comfortable with the person that I was, not who I was becoming. As I evolved, their impression of me did not; and I no longer fit their paradigm. Who I was could no longer coexist with who I was becoming.

I don't fault everyone for gravitating away from my life. Grief does not make you the most pleasant person at times, and sometimes people pull away because they don't know how to help you. When someone says, "you have changed" although well-meaning it can be used as a manipulative tactic to guilt you into being the person that they were comfortable with. It's easier for them to try to force you to be the person they once knew when everything was "normal", and you were "happy". People said to me, "you've changed" or "you're different," and for a time while I was still working through the need for acceptance, I would allow guilt to revert me to the person they once knew. After a while, I stopped feeling guilty and defensive, and I started accepting the fact that I HAD changed, I WAS different. How could I not be? Death changes you, suicide changes you, grief changes you, tragedy changes you. I had seen the man that I loved for 17 years die with a self-inflicted gun wound to his head. He bled out, open and wounded in front of me, and I was bleeding out, open and wounded in front of the world.

I've made plenty mistakes in the process of my grieving. I'm sure I've overcompensated with my kids trying to make everything feel normal again. I've made daily mistakes because I was not honest with myself about where I was mentally and what I could feasibly handle. Superwoman had run into some devastating Kryptonite, and I'm sure I picked up some bad coping mechanisms. But it is all a part of my process. God is patient with me and continues to hold my hand through the fire. He is right there in the furnace with me as I walk this path and those things that are not healthy are being burned away. As the smoke clears, I am left with more and more of my authentic self to present to the world.

As I am navigating through my sixth year of widowhood, this is definitely a bittersweet moment of victory. It's unquestionably hard to reconcile the fact that many of the gains I have made in my life would not have come about without many of the losses the past six years have handed me. Some may even describe my past six years as a series of Pyrrhic Victories; and in many ways, I am inclined to agree. I don't know why I had to lose so much to gain my true self, but in the words of Marvin Sapp "Here I am, I'm still standing."

So, I say to you, the reader, the widow who may not know who she is without her husband because life has ushered you from "us" to "me".

You will regain ground.

You will start over.

When people say, "you've changed" just simply answer, "you're right."

Those changes may be good, bad, ugly, or indifferent (usually it's all of the above) and people have every right to choose whether or not they want to engage with the changed you and different you. But as long as you are not intentionally hurtful, let people say what they're going to say, and continue to allow God to do what's He's going to do in your life.

Six years ago, I could not answer the questions: "Who are you?" and "Where do you see yourself in five years?" I couldn't even see past the current day. Are things perfect? Not in the least. But I have peace, joy, a new path, and new direction. I see a future for my children and me. Although unfortunately, it does not include my late husband and some of the people I thought would be in my life forever, what it does include is us. What it does include is me.

This road is full of hills and valleys. The hills are small, and the valleys can be deep. But today, I thank God that I am in a good place. I'm very busy with plans that are my own: I have completed my doctoral degree in Curriculum and Instruction, I have recently completed seminary, (earning my Bachelors in Biblical Studies), I currently work two jobs (full-time special-education teacher and part-time special education professor), I travel, I've made my own network of friends, I've launched a nonprofit organization - Dialogos, which is a postvention organization for families affected by suicide, I have plans to become a Chaplain and specialize in crises, trauma, grief, and loss, and finally, I am dating (and do desire to be married again).

When you find your authentic identity, you stop looking to belong; you stop looking to fit in because you have an understanding that God is going to place the people in your life that are supposed to be there. You have an understanding that God is going to place you where you are supposed to be. You don't have to chase anyone, and you don't have the beg anyone to be in your life. Those from my past that have accepted me through my metamorphosis are the people that are supposed to enter the next phase of my life with me. During my process, I moved to a city called Novi. Novi means "The New Place" and "The Ninth Month". For a while, I tried to hold onto people that had no problem letting go of me. I've since stopped trying to build and birth old things in new places.

I still own that vision board. When I look upon that woman with the blank face, I no longer see a woman that is void of identity. I look at the brush that hovers over her and sees a blank canvas full of possibilities, ready to be painted into whoever SHE wants to be. Not to create beauty, she was born beautiful. But to present to the world a face defined in full color. She now spreads her butterfly wings in the full radiance of who she truly is:

No longer afraid to shine.

No longer afraid to fly.

And you shouldn't be either.

Chapter 4

The Hustle and Flow of Khadija Ali: A Black Woman's State of Mental Health

I lost my husband of sixteen years to colon cancer on August 13, 2007. "Ali," as he was affectionately known, transitioned early that Monday morning right after his nurse and I had bathed him. Once we'd changed his clothes and turned him over, he took one final deep breath, and he was gone. I didn't consider my state of mind then. There was so much to do.

The Background

In 2004, a routine physical as part of his job (he was a firefighter) turned out in a way neither of us imaged. Through a colonoscopy, the doctors discovered cancer. Two-and-a-half-years after his diagnosis, he died, but Ali had been so young and vibrant for so long. He died at only thirty-seven years old. He had gone from a thin but healthy muscular physique to being skinny and emaciated. He was in so much pain that there was nothing I could do for him to take the pain away. I felt so helpless and terrified.

But, like many black women, I hid those emotions. Besides, I had to gather myself and be strong for my husband.

A few days before Ali passed, we were at the hospital. I remember seeing Dr. Condemi, his oncologist, walk our way. Dread overcame me. I knew what he was going to say, and he said it.

"There's nothing else I can do for him," he said.

My heart beat as if it was going to jump out of my chest. Inside, I was mortified and shocked, but I couldn't show those emotions. Sadness had covered Ali's face, and I didn't want him to worry if I was okay.

"What are you worried about?" Dr. Condemi asked him.

There, staring death in the face, he said, "My wife and children."

I promised Ali, then and there, that I was okay and that I would take care of our children. "Don't worry about anything," is what I said out loud. But inside, my world fell apart. I wanted to scream and hit his doctor for delivering such awful news, but I couldn't allow Ali to see me fall apart and know there was nothing he could do to fix it. He had always been the voice of reason and leader in our family, and that day, he passed the baton on to me. It was a job I did not want but knew I had to take on.

I left the hospital and called my best friend and grandmother. They attempted to console me through my hysterical tears in the best way they could.

"Be strong," was my grandmother's advice. "Wipe your tears."

Although my best friend couldn't relate to my pain or fear, she offered her perspective on what she would do if it had been her husband.

I hung up the phone. Numbness seeped into my body. Right then, I decided to put on a brave face for my husband and children and to keep my sanity.

He died a few days later, and I alerted everyone by phone. Every time I uttered the words, it felt like a stab in the back. Every call, every sentence shattered me like glass. I'd hang up, collapse into my friend Debi's arms, and cry. Then, when it was time to make another call, I'd don my "mask" and press forward.

At the time of Ali's death, we were homeless and living house-to-house. We had struggled to maintain in the midst of his illness. I had no time to "fall apart." There was no time. I had to keep my family moving forward. His death scared and angered me. I was in shock as well, but I hid my emotions from my children. I'd drink a bottle of Moscato every night before drifting off to scattered fits of sleep. The room would have to be spinning from my point-of-view before I felt comfortable enough to go to sleep. My crying took place only when the children were in bed, or I was alone in the car.

I suffered in silence

During the day, I, "Super Black Woman," took my kids to school, paid bills, and tended to household chores. I made it happen! I put on a front because I had to. My "hustle" came from the realization that there were no

26

strong arms to catch me anymore when I fell into in those dark moments of despair. "Super Black Woman" meant I'd watched my mother and grandmother be single mothers, and I believed, on a subconscious level, this was what I needed to do to survive. The narrative of our people has always been one that we are and were survivors. I know that black women especially wear strength like a badge of honor, but deep down inside, I felt anything but strong.

The Breakdown

A couple of days before Thanksgiving, I was on my way to school, and I started crying uncontrollably. I got to school and sat in the parking lot thinking that I was losing my mind. I called a few friends sobbing incoherently. Each one asked me, "What's wrong?"

"I don't know," was my response.

Finally, a friend suggested that I visit my school counselor and ask for help. I got out of the car and headed straight to my counselor's office. She was familiar with my story and suggested that I go to Bergen Pines, a mental health hospital not far away from the school. I agreed to go, and in that ten-minute drive, I decided that I was going to quit trying to do things myself. I told myself I would do everything they told me to do no matter what. I didn't care what would happen to my children. The state would take them, or family members would intervene. A strange calmness and resolve came over me during that ride, however, when I arrived at the hospital, it was a different story.

My school counselor had given me a note to give to the person I would be meeting, but when I got to the room, there was no one there. I turned around and found the information desk where they informed me that there was no one in that building by the name on the paper. They advised me to go to the emergency room to get assistance.

In the emergency room, I received the same answer: nobody by that name was there, either. I was baffled. At that point, I left the emergency room, got back in my car, and went home.

Looking back on the situation, I can see God's plan for me was not to give up, but at the time, I was truly puzzled on what that experience was all about.

I would go on, of course, because that's what "strong women" do. They. Go. On.

Although I tried to block out and rationalize the grief, my body had other plans. I experienced panic attacks, vertigo, and sensitivity to light. I walked around with sunglasses on during the day to shield my eyes from the sun and the glaring lights in the classroom at school. My mind was in a fog. Clarity only existed when I got my children to school and attended classes.

I never shared the physical symptoms I was suffering from with anyone. How could I fall apart?

My husband had truly been the only one to be there for me when I was sick, and now he was dead.

One day I woke up dizzy and could barely function. It scared me enough to get to the emergency room. At first, I didn't tell anyone I was there, but I kept hearing my husband's voice urging me to call someone. I phoned my brother-in-law. About thirty minutes later, he showed up with his cousin Mona in tow. After being there for a couple of hours, I was discharged. I'd been diagnosed with dehydration and vertigo. I had obtained a prescription to keep the dizziness away, but all it did was make me nauseous. Never once did I attribute my symptoms to grief, nor did I think that it would manifest in my body.

I resumed life as usual with the same pattern: household chores, tending to my children, and settling my husband's estate. At night, I let loose in my grief. I'd spent countless hours scouring the Internet looking for people like me: widowed and confused. Facebook didn't exist back then, and there were no online support groups like there are now. I eventually found the "Young Widowed Bulletin Board" and spent my nights reading numerous threads about widows feeling crazy, angry, or drinking themselves into oblivion. Reading them gave me immense comfort. What I was experiencing was real and valid.

Interestingly enough, I was still seeing my counselor, Lynn. She was someone my husband and I had both been going to for marital counseling before he passed away. After he died, I continued to see her. I hoped she could provide some answers as to what I was feeling and how to cope with those feelings. At the time, I was ignorant to the idea of a grief counselor. It never dawned on me to find one. I genuinely thought that people around me could help me through this process.

Lynn did the best she could and recommended I see a psychiatrist for my anxiety and depression. The psychiatrist was a black woman, so I naively thought she would be helpful and understand my pain. I quickly learned that a psychiatrist's primary role is to monitor medications and that's it. My sessions with her were brief and unfulfilling. To top it off, I was paying out-of-pocket, and her visits were not cheap. She had prescribed some medications to keep the anxiety manageable and the depression at bay. I felt they were only temporary fixes to the real issue: grief.

Reflecting back on those times, I believe I intuitively knew there was something deeper going on with me than anxiety and depression. Don't get me wrong; I had always battled with both issues on and off since I was fifteen years old. I didn't seek treatment for either until I became an adult.

What I couldn't ever get anyone to understand was the deep, gaping hole that existed inside my soul. I couldn't describe the desensitized state I walked around in for weeks or why I was angry at my husband, at God, and at people in general.

Why did my husband have to die?

What about our children who needed their daddy?

How was it possible for my daughter with Down's syndrome to miss out on the love and protection of her father?

It was so unfair!

None of the counselors, doctors, or school staff had answers to those questions. And the community that was so loving towards our family before and during my husband's illness and death avoided my children like the plague after his passing.

I was isolated too, partly because my friends and family couldn't understand what it was like to lose your better half. When I did open up and express the depths of my pain, many wouldn't listen. His best friend told me once, "Be thankful that you had time with him."

To be honest, I wanted to slap him for saying that and being insensitive and dismissive to a wife who was grieving.

Religion and Grief

The Islamic community that I belonged to with my husband also didn't have anything in place for grieving wives and children. And, although the Qur'an instructs Muslims to take care of the widow and orphans, no one within the community took on the responsibility of providing for us.

In essence, we were left to fend for ourselves.

This is very controversial for me to say or admit, but it is the truth. I found then, and still find now, certain subjects such as death are dealt with as a one-time event in religious communities. There is no comfort or concern to the wives and children left behind. I became the head of household. I had to keep my family going and myself sane.

I know of a few widows who never recovered from their spouse's passing. Many wound up on drugs, in mental health facilities, or even in prison. I can see why. I almost became a statistic. I abused drugs and alcohol (in secret) and almost checked myself into a mental health hospital. The stress of losing a spouse for the average American is statistically staggering.

It is my belief that a Black woman experiences grief at higher rates than other groups in America. We already have some of the highest rates of obesity, certain cancers, and heart disease. Add grief to that equation, and the percentage is astounding. I gained more than seventy pounds since my husband's death and did not attend grief counseling until recently. It has been ten years since his passing and I suppressed a lot of my grief due to the "strong, Black woman" syndrome. I have even had several conversations with my grandmother who is twice widowed.

She said, "You don't need counseling. You need to pray."

"Grandma, I pray every day," I told her. "I still need someone to talk to about how I feel."

There is a numbness amongst black people when it comes to mental health. It is almost as if we are afraid to admit we need to seek help in our mental faculties. Ironically, many of us will go to our primary care doctors and do whatever they ask, and take whatever medications they say are good for our bodies-- no questions asked.

But for some mind-boggling reason, we do not equate mental health as being equally as important.

So how did I finally find true closure with Ali's passing?

Grief counseling.

Over the course of six sessions, I felt heard and validated. And, for the first time since Ali's passing, I was able to properly process my grief without judgment, ridicule, or dismissal, thanks to a special friend, Christina Saunders, who encouraged me to go. I was initially resistant because I didn't want to open up old wounds. But what I found was that in order for those wounds to truly heal, I needed to be vulnerable and acknowledge them.

In my last counseling session, I wrote a letter to Ali which said the one thing I hadn't said in ten years: Goodbye.

Chapter 5

The Hustle and Flow of Cheryl Barnes: Rebuilding Me After His Hustle Ended

How it Began

I had always been the nerdy girl who read and studied all the time through high school and into college. My nose was stuck in a book most time and reading helped me to earn great grades.

But, on the other hand, it did not win me any popularity contests or a boyfriend.

So, I spent my time alone, working, studying, and reading. No one really wanted to hang out with the nerdy girl unless it had to do with study tips, notes, or help with papers.

It didn't help I didn't consider myself attractive. But, like any other girl growing into adulthood, there was one thing I really and truly wanted: to be loved for *me*. I had always pictured a man who would sweep me off my feet, marry me and love and care for me all my days. In return, he would have every bit of my heart.

No one seemed interested in that side of me, and so I silently cried as I watched nearly all my friends getting engaged or married. That all changed when I met Tony. We worked at the same dorm for work-study, so I saw him every day. He was so gorgeous with a huge smile and gigantic shoulders. He was my type of man, but I never thought he would look my way. But look my way he did, and my heart skipped a beat.

I was done. Apparently, so was he.

We became inseparable and loved each other like we could have loved no other. He treated me like I was precious, and I most certainly felt the same about him. Even after marrying him. I could hardly believe he wanted *me* – the nerdy, kind-of-chubby girl. But he thought I was beautiful and spent his life trying to convince me of it. He saw me with his heart -- the same way I saw him. That was what our love was like.

Not to say we didn't battle - we surely did. But love and the feeling of belonging to one another overpowered any anger we felt in those moments.

All through our marriage, I tried to be what I felt a good wife should be. I took care of the home, the kids, the basic household things. I worked, of course, but Tony was the primary breadwinner. It served his male ego (and my sensibilities) for us to have that arrangement. We shared many things too: decisions about major expenses and our two boys, trips we would take, where we should move, etc. We moved through our lives this way, having our ups and downs all the while, but deep down, we were quite happy. Tony had earned his Master's in Social Work, and it was about to be my turn to further my education by attending nursing school.

Then, the bottom fell out of all our plans.

A former athlete and the picture of health and fitness, Tony was diagnosed with end-stage renal failure most likely caused by lupus. At first, neither one of us had any idea what that meant. But, being the reader and researcher that I am, I asked a lot of questions and researched the Internet. Phrases like, "Lupus is worse in men" and "End Stage Renal Failure mostly results in death without a transplant," jumped off the screen.

"Not for us," I told myself. "We will be the exception to the rule."

***

So began my hustle.

I went to Tony's doctor's appointments with him, took notes, and asking plenty of questions. I learned about every single medication he was on when he had to take it, and for what reason. We sat together at his dialysis sessions, and I questioned the technicians about the procedure. And, for a brief time, we did dialysis at home. I was the main person to handle that.

I read about special diets for kidney patients and adapted the whole family's lifestyle in support of my husband's health. I knew more about him and his health than anyone. Notebook after notebook filled with the information I'd learned. Then, I studied ways to help him physically and mentally cope with his illness and treatment.

During all of this, I tried to maintain a semblance of normalcy in our lives.

"This is how I am going to save my family," I thought. "If I work hard enough, if I hustle hard enough, he is going to survive this, and we can get back to our regular lives."

Oh, I knew the disease would shorten his life, but I just knew, because of his strength and stubbornness and my hard work, he was going to survive.

However, he started suffering some serious complications such as seizures, which I never knew about until the day he fell and broke his neck in the midst of one. Immediately after the surgery to repair his neck, he began to suffer constant seizures which forced the doctors to put him into a medical coma. While he lay in a coma, my days took on a new rhythm: see the kids to school, visit with Tony at the hospital, go to work, go back to the hospital, then go home to mother my boys. This became my daily routine, with slight variations depending on the situation, ultimately for the rest of his life. The *strong black woman* had arrived on the scene and was taking no prisoners.

He did wake from the coma, but he was not the same. The months he spent in bed recuperating after the coma had weakened his body, the seizures had damaged his brain. But still, I was determined to get my family and get my husband back. He was released and briefly rehabilitated, but he was not getting *his* hustle back. So, I continued my hustle: researching, demanding that the doctors do more (or explain why they could not) while working, paying bills and loving my boys. It was as if Tony and I switched our roles; he needed me to take care of him more and more. I did it because I loved him and he did need me. I could see in his eyes how proud he was to have a wife like me - a wife who was willing to fight for him.

The hospitalizations and doctor's appointments became more frequent, and I worked as hard as I could with the weight of all the burdens I was carrying, but understandably, my mind started to slip a bit and so did my work. My employer became less and less understanding of this. Instead of asking what I needed to keep up, he threatened to fire me if I didn't "shape up". I continued to work as hard as I could and stay focused. My employer reduced my work until I was basically a secretary when I had been a supervisor. This was too much to bear. My job was the one place I could feel I had some control and success, but no longer. I resigned my position. At the time, we had enough money for me to take a month off to rest and spend more time with my family, have longer visits with Tony and enjoy fun activities with the boys. I felt so relaxed - I wished my life could have stayed that way. However, money was running out. At the exact moment I was getting concerned, I received a phone call from a former co-worker who gave me a lead for a new job. Thankfully, it was a company my old company had done business with so I knew the management very well. This job was a more compassionate atmosphere and gave me the flexibility to take care of Tony or the boys if need be, without side-eye glances from managers.

Tony continued to weaken, and I continued to hustle. The hustle became a way of life for me. As I hustle, it was a very smooth flow to my life. I didn't even have to think about it anymore, that's how smooth it was. Everyone needed me, so I was going to be there for everyone. People often asked me, then and now, what about his family, friends? I say, this is my family, and it means more to me than anyone, so I never expected help. I never really got it either. No matter. I kept it moving.

By this time, Tony had spent one-and-a-half years away from home in hospitals and rehab centers. I fought hard to get him home. I was certain he wasn't thriving because he wasn't home with his family. So, I began to push him to think positive about healing and the future, while I pushed the medical professionals to figure out how to make him better. I pushed myself just as hard to get answers and handle everything else I was responsible for. The hustle began to wear me out, but I didn't realize it until much, much later.

I finally got him home the summer of 2014. I was so very happy-finally, I had achieved part of my goal. But things were not better for Tony - by now, he needed total care. I could not afford a private nurse to help, so the tasks of caring for my husband fell to me and on occasion, my sons. We went on this way throughout that summer. I learned even more about his care, especially about caring for the terrible wound he had on his tailbone, caused by months in bed. The days took on another rhythm, starting with me rising at 5:45 am to give him his first medications of the day to fall into bed by 11:30 pm. I was tired, but this was my family, and I was going to do it because they were important to me.

In late August, he suddenly spiked a fever on a Tuesday morning. He was quite lethargic, so I called an ambulance and prepared myself for yet another hospital stay. It had become so commonplace for me that I wasn't the slightest bit worried and even joked a bit with Tony as we waited for the ambulance. As I soon found out, this time was different. He nearly died in the ER, and he seemed to sink before my eyes. The last week of his life, he spent most of the time unconscious. The one day he improved enough to say anything, he said to me, "I love you, I want to go home, I love you" over and over again. I treasure that. It made every bit of the hustle worth it for me.

At one point it was made clear that all of the medications he was getting and all of the machines he was hooked to were not helping him. Tony and I made a decision about all of that long time ago, so I forced myself to honor it. Tony fought dying as hard as he could. He battled the respirator, thrashing his head on his pillow. He didn't want to leave our boys. I knew that so I put both of my hands on his face and whispered, "It's okay, honey. I don't want you to hurt anymore, so this is what we are doing. If you can do it without the meds, I would be so happy. But if you can't, I understand. It's breaking my heart, and I don't want you to go, but I understand if you have to. My heart is breaking, but we will make it. Don't worry; I'll make it."

Then he relaxed and let himself go, all the while I was holding his face in my hands. I watched the monitors counting his breaths and heartbeats start to slow. I stared at it like I could "will" it to speed up. After a time, the nurse put her fingers to his neck and said, "He's gone."

I asked the nurses to remove his tubes and lines so our boys could see him again without those tethers that ultimately did him no good. I left the room while they did this for us. My cousins, who had just happened to come to town, sat with me in the lobby as the tears rolled silently. I sat with him for another hour or so, trying to understand what just happened. Even more so, I was trying to wrap my head around the fact that I was leaving him there and not coming back to see him the next day and that I would never hear him call my name or say, "I love you" ever again.

The Funeral

As I had done before, I took care of Tony and his arrangements myself. My in-laws helped me with money for it, but the planning was all me, and it's what he would have wanted. The whole thing was surreal; who knew I would be in a funeral home, arguing about who gets mentioned in a funeral program for my husband, let alone sitting there and planning the horrible thing? I was in a daze. I didn't belong there. *Why am I here?* I had thought. I wanted to see him. *If I saw him, maybe he wasn't dead*, I thought to myself over and over.

Many of Tony's relatives came to the service, and I embraced them all, but thinking to myself, *where were you all before?* Then I decided: they are here now, and they are promising to be here for us going forward. However, after the service, everyone went home and back to their lives. The boys and I were left alone. I slowly packed up the medical supplies that I used to care for Tony. I couldn't look at them anymore. I had all of these things, I had all of this knowledge, and yet, I still failed in my hustle to save my beloved. The hustle failed me. I still couldn't believe it. As hard as I worked during that time, Tony still died. My boys no longer had a father, and I had lost my strong, handsome, loving husband. I was beyond furious.

I began to think: what was the point? I cared so much and it...just...didn't...matter. He died anyway. I was angry.

Grief Books Didn't Help Me

I bought and tried to read any book on grief I could lay my hands on, searching for an answer, any answer to why this happened. I joined a grief support group, but I think since I was the youngest in the group; I really didn't fit in. So, I tried to "cure" my grief myself by swimming in my feelings. I immersed myself in my anger and pain. Along with the anger, came the intense guilt. I couldn't save him because I didn't work hard enough? Racked with these feelings, I decided to let my anger carry me through life. I was angry at almost everyone, in particular, God. As a result of my intense anger, I started using my widowhood as a weapon:

"Don't talk to me today. I'm in my feelings because I'm a widow."
"I don't want to go. I'm widowed, and I don't feel like it."

"You there! Stop laughing. Nothing's funny. Especially my life, because my husband died."

"Oh, I forgot to pay that bill because I'm a widow. You should be more understanding."

"Why are you calling me? I'm widowed, and I don't feel like talking to you at all."

I made many statements like this and felt perfectly justified. After all, it was true, right? I was devastated at the loss of my Tony. Everyone needed to understand that and not bother me. I was angry for months.

The only people I wasn't angry with were our boys. I took great pains to not take things out on them. After all, they were gifts my husband left me, and I loved them. I watched over them carefully as my husband would have expected from me. However, those boys, especially my oldest, were acutely aware that I was suffering. They became quite perceptive and knew when to leave Mom alone.

Leave Me Alone

Leave me alone, I screamed inside my head almost hourly. I was alone and trying to cope with being a single parent and all that entails with it. I continued to hustle, but there was nothing behind it except keeping things afloat for the boys. As the reality of truly being alone sank in, my anger and aggressive behavior gave way to depression. I didn't realize I was depressed. I knew I was grieving very deeply and the few people who stayed in contact with me encouraged me to work out those feelings. I didn't want to leave the house except to take care of necessities; especially nothing social-related. My husband's family and many of the friends who promised to be there for us also completely disappeared. The few times I tried to take my friends up on their previous offers to do things together was always met with "I'm busy this weekend. I will let you know when I'm free and we will get together, I promise." That happened so often that I just gave up trying. It wasn't worth it to me to keep chasing people. As a result, I became a bigger hermit than I already was.

I was angry, but I was also very depressed. So depressed, in fact, I considered taking myself out of the game entirely. I was tired from the years of caring for everyone and not being cared for. I was missing my husband quite badly. Life held no excitement for me. I considered just going to sleep and not waking up. The only thing that kept me from doing that was the thought that my kids would have to deal with losing another parent. I knew they needed me and I needed them. So, I began to make some efforts to pick myself up again.

I tried many things to help me work through my pain. I never answered my phone. I didn't want talk to anyone about anything. That was the easiest part for me. I bought things I didn't really need. I ate things I shouldn't have eaten in the quantities I was eating them. I read every book about grieving that I could and joined many widow groups, searching for relief from my hurt. I kept trying to read those books on grief, but I wasn't able to find solace in any of those activities. I slept *a lot*. I was alone, lonely and sad and no one seemed to care about that. I was even told that I needed to shake it off for the good of my children. In the midst of it all, I forced myself to get back to school and take some online courses. I did well in them - made the President's list in fact. But even that brought me no real joy.

I was such an incredible mess...and no one seemed to notice or even care.

My Mental Health

I decided, for the good of the boys, to see a doctor and find out how many things were wrong with me. She diagnosed me with chronic depression, a Vitamin D deficiency and a distinct lean toward diabetes. The depression rung true for me as I realized that I had been this way for several months and it was affecting everything. She prescribed me an antidepressant which was supposed to help certain chemicals in my brain start working again. After a few weeks, I did feel myself begin to lift from the fog I was in. Smiling stopped hurting my face so much. My anger was slowly drifting away. It wasn't a miracle cure, but it was a start, and it helped me decide it was time to get myself back into life. I wasn't exactly sure how that would work, but I felt it was time to try.

I started by looking for a new job. The place where I was working was becoming a less compassionate and less friendly place to work, so I decided it was time to move on from there. I found another job and began having some measure of success with it almost immediately. I actually felt happy to go to work to be with my co-workers. Best of all, there were several people there who had experienced loss, and being able to relate to others on that level was so helpful and made me feel less alone.

I spent a lot of time on Facebook. I belonged to several widow groups, and I was able to express my pain and anger there. But, again, something was missing for me, other than having obvious interaction with people in similar situations as myself. I found that expressing my feelings in writing gave me a voice I didn't have in "real life." Using this voice gave me some semblance of relief that I hadn't felt since Tony died. The number of "likes" and comments about how eloquently I wrote about my experiences put an idea in my head. When Tony was in his coma, I began writing a blog to work out my feelings and frustration over Tony's illness. I only made a couple of entries in it. Reading them again, and at the same time, making connections with other widow bloggers, inspired me to start my writing again.

After taking Tony's advice from long ago, "Girl, you should write for a living. You are so good at it," I told myself that life is full of risks and that I would never know until I tried. I named my blog, Widowness and Light. For me, it fits. "Widowness" is a term I created. It developed from the hustle and bustle of life since his death.

My blog has met with a very small measure of popularity, but that isn't what matters to me. My blog began as my voice to grief and pain. Since I really didn't have very many friends, and even fewer willing to listen to me work out my pain, I wrote my feelings out and published them for others to read. The response I received was amazing. So many widowed people told me that they could hear themselves in my writing and that they knew exactly what I felt because they felt the same way. I began to feel as though I was helping people again.

I feel as though my writing is slowly pulling me from my shell, where I've been hiding underneath my pain. It has given me the confidence to reach out to people I never would have before and to say things I would never have said. I have never had a problem expressing my feelings, but I am learning not to let them overwhelm me and pull me under like as before. I feel as though I am fulfilling a promise to myself to continue helping people who need it. Sharing with the world how I work my way through "widowness" is my way of helping others. Along the way, I have met many others who have been through the pain that I have been through. Knowing that I am not alone in this life of widowing has had a positive effect on my life.

My New Hustle

The hustle had begun again, but with a different rhythm and flow. My new hustle and flow is benefiting everyone around me, as the old one benefited primarily my family. I think Tony smiles down at me, watching me work while saying, "That's my baby. I knew she could do it."

Many widows think that because they have experienced an incredible loss, they have become weakened. I felt this way, too. When we lose someone, either through illness, accident, suicide or even by natural means, it is a test of our strength. I looked back over the years I spent taking care of my husband and our boys and realized, I carry a great deal of strength and power. That strength and power come from love and nothing else. I was able to reach deep within myself and do what had to be done. You will be different because of the loss, sure, but your strength never leaves you. Remember that. Your strength and power, born of love, never goes away.

Chapter 6

The Hustle and Flow of Kerry Phillips: Broken Crayons Still Color

What now?

I stared into the mirror trying to make sense of how I'd gotten to this place. To this place of immense sorrow, uncertainty, and heartbreak. To this place where my faith was questioned, and I was disappointed in God.

I was 32 years old and what was supposed to be a year of newlywed bliss and all the giddiness of young love had turned into death, grief, and mourning.

The man I'd loved almost since the day we met – nearly ten years ago – was gone. There was no cancer diagnosis, no drunken driver or on the job accident. It was a tiny little mosquito that upended my life. An insect so small I could crush it with one swat yet it crushed me instead. Everything was taken from me. All my plans...my dreams...my goals....my heart.

It had been a year and six days since I stood in front of practically all the people I held near and dear to exchange wedding vows. There was something magical in the air that no one could quite put his/her finger on. Looking back, it seemed God knew my husband was on borrowed time and gave me the gift of unadulterated happiness and love on our special day; a memory that would bring me comfort after his passing.

It was a typical Sunday morning. Church then the grocery store then back home to cook. My husband was in Guyana and had been battling what we thought was the flu for the past few days. I hesitated to call him because it was 7 a.m. as I thought he'd probably be asleep. I figured I'd just call when I returned home.

That's the thing with us as human beings. We always think we have more time. We put off saying I love you. We put off that vacation. We put off the little things only to realize in the end they were big things.

I regret not making that call but have convinced myself that perhaps it was for the best. Maybe it was better that his last words to me were, "I love you." Words I could forever treasure. Words he knew would sustain me through my darkest days.

Less than 12 hours since we last spoke, I returned to my car from church service to a flurry of text messages and missed calls. Before I could even make sense of the texts, my phone rang. And just like that, my life forever changed when my father-in-law said words no young, newlywed should ever have to hear: your husband has died.

How does someone who had just prayed, just worshipped, just sat and listened as the pastor preached about God's love, get news like this? News like this while sitting in the church parking lot...news like this when she's surrounded by others, oblivious to her pain...news like this without her husband to be there to help her make sense of those four words.

I can't remember crying when I initially got the news. It takes the body a while to process the information. It was too much for my brain to handle. How does a physically active, healthy 35-year-old just die? It was too beautiful a day to have such a horrific ending. I was too in love to have to say goodbye. It was a misunderstanding. It had to be. I dialed his number, hoping he'd be confused by my panic and reassure me all was well. The phone just kept ringing...

The next few days and weeks were a blur. I dutifully coordinated the return of his body – that's how they referred to him...the body (the man who loved life more than anyone I'd ever met; the person who could light up a room simply by walking in; and the man who made me laugh until my sides and face hurt was reduced to "the body"). From making funeral arrangements stateside to coordinating airline tickets for out-of-town guests, it seemed I was on autopilot.

As I scratched item after item off my to-do list, the reality of my husband's death started taking its toll. My already small frame was reduced to one I didn't recognize. Then if the physical reaction to his death wasn't bad enough, the thoughts started. The ones that make you wonder why God didn't take you too...why you were left here to grieve forever.

My husband and I dated long distance, and I would always joke that no matter where in the world he was, I'd always get to him. This time, I couldn't. I didn't even know where he was. Was he in heaven? Was he simply asleep in his grave awaiting Christ's return? I didn't know where he was, but my heart wanted to get to him, regardless of where he was.

Looking back, I don't think I was suicidal. I just wanted the pain of his death to be lifted. I wanted to not feel hollow. I wanted to escape from the nightmare that had become my "new" life.

Then there were the dreams. I'd be searching for him, begging for him to reveal his whereabouts so I could bring him back. Back to his family. Back to his kids. Back to me. Most times I wouldn't find him, but sometimes he'd come to me. He'd tell me they were all wrong; he wasn't dead. He'd often tell me he had simply been in the hospital recuperating. The doctors had screwed up, and he was alive waiting for me to figure it all out. I'd cry and tell him how much I missed him…how much I love him. And just like the real world where he was taken suddenly, I'd wake up. I'd be so happy at first, knowing he was alive and that he was okay. Then my brain would snap back to reality.

Remember you brought him home? You saw him at the funeral home, right? You touched him. You felt his skin. You ran your fingers through his locs. You have to know he's not coming back. You were dreaming. He's no longer alive.

That's the worst part: when you have to relive the death over and over again. You have to feel the same shock, the same pain, the same hurt, the same raw emotions.

Not only had I lost my husband but I lost my dreams and goals as well. Every plan and desire I had was intertwined with his. My entire world was built around his vision. We'd move to the Caribbean, open an internet café, perhaps a boutique or a juice bar. In order for our future to be successful, it needed both of us. We complemented each other in so many ways. He was the bold extrovert while I worked my magic behind the scenes. We were an unstoppable pair.

But now that life had come to screeching halt; I was lost. I was alone with no game plan. My "we" was now just "me".

Which brings me back to "*what now?*"

I had to figure out how I'd get back into the land of the living. I was tired of just going through the motions, putting on a brave face while secretly crumbling inside. My shower was my refuge. It was my place to cry, think, pray, strategize, and talk to both God and my husband.

Unlike many widows who complain about family and friends who aren't there for them, my loved ones were consistently there for me though I kept them at arm's length. I'm very much an introvert and my grieving needed to be a personal process. I needed to make sense of my loss – if there is such a thing – and find out who I was without my husband. *Would I be the person who died upon my husband's death or would I be the person who lived in spite of?*

One of the perks of being an introvert is that your "circle" tends to be rather small. For me, that meant there weren't many people I needed to tell about my husband's passing. As for social media, my friends knew not to tag us in any posts or offer any condolences online. I was perfectly content with the rest of the world continuing to believe I was happily married.

Despite my anger at God, I faithfully attended church each week. One Sunday the sermon was about how as Christians we think we're immune to life's storm and that we needed to remember that there was never a promise made to us by God. It was on that Sunday that my anger – anger I'd held onto for over three years – began to subside. I let go of the feeling of entitlement, where I assumed I was only deserving of blessings because I was a "good" person. Though I served a perfect God, I was not a saint. I was no more deserving of God's grace and mercy than anyone else.

The pastor also spoke of God's love for us and that it was during difficult times that we should turn to Him. As he preached, I begin to think about the poem, "Footprints in the Sand". The well-known story tells of a man who questions God, asking why the Lord had forsaken him at the most trying times in his life as evidenced by one set of footprints in the sand. It is later revealed that it was because God had been carrying him during these moments.

After the sermon that day, my prayer shifted. It was no longer about "why": why my husband died or why this happened to me. Instead, my prayer was for healing and strength; prayers to make it through the storm. I asked God to walk me through my grief and help me grow. Help me find my way and learn to walk in my purpose. I needed Him to show me how I could be better for having gone through such a tragic ordeal. And, though I wouldn't let my family and friends in, I knew they were praying for me too.

As I worked through my grief, the thought of dating post-loss began to swirl in my head. I'd sworn that I would never love again, but the reality was that I was now only 35 years old. The thought of never having companionship and being alone for the rest of my life didn't seem so appealing.

I had questions about dating as a widow but no one to turn to for answers. I didn't know any other young widows. Members of my "circle" were either married, in committed long-term relationships or busy trying to navigate the world of dating themselves – without having a "W" stamped to their chest.

After looking around online, there weren't many resources available. Many members in the groups I'd found were still in the hole in which I'd just come out of. I no longer wanted to die. I didn't want death to get a "bonus" spouse, one who willingly gave up on life and allow death to claim her too. That darkness was behind me. Prayers had brought me to a place of light. I was happy and seeking my joy.

I decided to create my own support group and Young, Widowed & Dating was founded in November 2015. It would be a place for those further along in the grief journey. I needed a place where death was not the central theme. It had to be known that there is light on the other side of the tunnel. I wanted it to be a supportive environment for young widows and widowers who, despite a piece of them dying, knew there was life left in them. What started as a vision soon became a special community for those working to get to that "other side" of loss.

I continued to work on my own healing, and now that I'd "met" others who were in my situation, I felt less alone. Finally, someone understood what I was going through.

I started finding my voice as I served as the Administrator of the group. I noticed that although we all took different paths, we shared many of the same struggles and challenges. There had to be others, outside my tiny group (less than 100 members at the time) who needed to know they weren't alone.

In May of 2016, I felt empowered by my group and decided I was ready to share my story publicly. Don't' get me wrong; I was not "over" the loss. I don't think it's something one ever gets "over". You simply learn to live with a gaping hole in your heart. I wrote my story, how I'd lost my husband and the lessons I'd learned along the way. I stared at the article, happy to finally put my thoughts down on paper and again was brought back to that dreaded question, *"what now?"*. What were my plans for the article? Who was I going to share it with?

Then, I did something that antisocial people just don't do. I found the largest platform and I shared my story. I submitted the piece to Arianna Huffington. At the time, she was co-founder and editor-in-chief of The Huffington Post, once ranked as "the most powerful blog in the world".

Within ten days, Arianna responded and said that not only was the article, "Life Lessons of a Young Widow" worthy of being added to the website, but I should consider becoming a regular contributor. I was excited, but I was hesitant. *A regular contributor?* But I only had one article!

On May 16th, I clicked the "submit" button, and the article went live. I was so thrilled seeing my byline that I threw caution to the wind and shared the piece on my personal Facebook page. The world stood still as I wondered if I'd made the right decision. I questioned if I'd shared too much; if I'd revealed too much of my pain.

What seemed like an eternity went by, and my inbox lit up. It was a classmate reaching out to say she had no idea I'd lost my husband and was praying for me. Before I could finish replying to her, another message. Then another and another. People started sharing my article: friends, family, Facebook acquaintances. Everyone seemed to be reading and sharing it. Then a widow reached out. She thanked me for writing the article and for putting into words what she'd wanted to say. More widows reached out, each complimenting me for sharing my story, which was ultimately their story as well.

I was initially overwhelmed by the outpouring of responses. I wondered if I'd bared too much of my soul…put too much of my story "on front street". Then I came across an Iyanla Vanzant quote that struck a chord: "When you stand and share your story in an empowering way, your story will heal you, and your story will heal someone else."

She was right. The article was essential to my grieving process. I could no more take it back than I could bring back my husband. It was my truth. I was widowed at 32. I was hurting. My pain was real. I let go of my regrets and embraced the fact that my article was a positive thing. In sharing, I was helping others.

After the outpouring of comments from fellow widows, I decided I'd use my writing to advocate for the widowed community. It's a responsibility I hold near and dear to my heart. I am honored that the members of my group trust me with their hurt, anger, betrayal, frustrations, and fears. In telling their stories, it helps other widows and widowers to feel less alone. It makes us all connected when we find that our story, circumstances, and feelings are shared by others. Each time someone reads my article and says, "I thought I was alone before I read this," it validates his/her feelings.

I've been writing for more than a year, and this has been the biggest year of healing for me. There is power in helping others, even when you are broken. Please know however that I'm a strong advocate of the expression that you can't pour from an empty cup. You do need to take care of yourself and even reach out to a professional if need be. There is no shame in knowing you can't go it alone. I only find that you don't have to be "over" your grief to be of help to others.

Someone once told me that my husband died so I could be a voice for widows. I do not believe that. I would gladly give this up for my happily ever after with him. I'd walk away for even one more day. I simply felt broken and needed to let out my emotions. All the beauty that came as a result of my telling my story, openly and honestly, was a blessing. I choose to support fellow widows in spite of his death not because of it.

With each story I tell, I am healing. With each member of the YW&D who tells me how much my group means to them, I am healing. With each kind word I receive, I am healing. With each hug I receive from a fellow widow, I am healing.

My hustle has been giving back to the widowed community which in turn has caused my blessings to flow, my healing to flow, my joy to flow, my purpose to flow, newfound friendships to flow and most importantly, helped me to find my flow.

Chapter 7

The Hustle and Flow of Rhonda Butler: A Pastor's Wife's Bitterness of Black Tea

Where or how do I start?

How do I live life without the one person who consumed my living since high school?

My thrust into widowhood began the early morning hours of Feb. 12, 2015, fueled by a harsh, medical diagnosis eighteen years prior; a diagnosis whose depth was not noticeable to the naked eye. Nonetheless, I am now thirty or so months into this journey, and my stomach still takes a dip when I drive past the hospital.

The loss of him is like the bitterness of black tea, a flavor I avoid despite any apparent health benefits. Likewise, I struggle to understand the benefit of my life as a widow. I consider myself open, flexible, able to adapt to change with a bounce-back attitude despite circumstances life may present to me. My mother described me as a strange child. For thirty-seven years I was married to my best friend, my man, my confidant, the father of our four children and grandfather of our eight grandchildren. I miss my pastor and husband, Rev. William Butler, Jr.

"Let this cup pass from me, nevertheless, not as I will, but as thou wilt" - Matthew 26:39

Around the age of twelve is when we became acquainted. We enrolled in a weekly Sunday evening young people's training class at my home church. Honestly, we had very little to do with each other then, but time does have a way of bringing about change. Ours began the summer of 1974, our first date, a double date to be exact on Christmas Eve in 1977. He proposed six months later.

"He who finds a wife finds a good thing" - Proverbs 18:22

A few weeks before the expected delivery of our first born I witnessed my husband announce his acceptance of God's call to the preaching ministry. I knew I had married the son
of a preacher man, a young man aspiring to uphold Christian values and yes, I expected that we'd be that active young couple serving the Lord in a local church.

But, a pastor's wife?

He was always very vocal about not following in his father's footsteps; yet, I treasure even now the joy of having had witnessed his spiritual growth, love, and service to the Lord. Together, we labored raising our family while pastoring two churches over a twenty-eight-year period.

"For I know the plans I have for you" - Jeremiah 29:11

Over time, we shared some unexpected health challenges that strengthened our faith and love physically, intimately, and spiritually. In the Fall of 2000 he was diagnosed with the shingles virus, and soon after that, we faced his first major surgery. In hindsight, that surgery was a precursor of what was to come.

During our oldest son's first year of college, we received news that my husband's heart was fragile and that he should consider a heart transplant. I usually arrive home before he does, but on this day, I found him home sitting at the dining room table, head down with tears streaming down his face. He looked up at me and said, "It's not good, they said I'm dying." He pulled me toward him, and we hugged. We both cried. I pointed to his Bible as a reminder of God's Word and replied, "Yes, we all are dying every day, but whose report will we believe?" We prayed, and God answered...briefly.

Years passed and with each milestone, whether birthdays, anniversaries or holidays, we celebrated the love and care the Lord granted us. We had seemingly conquered and settled into our new life with his illness neatly tucked away. Most were unaware of the depth of his condition, including our children who at that time were between junior high and college.

Easter Sunday had begun like any other day, however, on this day three of our grandchildren were with us for the ride to Sunday School. During the thirty-minute ride, I sensed a slight agitation from my husband and assumed it was due to the rising wave of the chatterboxes in the back seat. When we arrived at the church, I directed the grandchildren to their class as the pastor made his way to his office and moments later, my momentum was soon interrupted by the sound of a hard fall, followed by shouting voices, "It's Pastor Butler!" My first thought was to remind the Lord that this was one of His most holy days on the Christian calendar and it shouldn't be interrupted. God had His plan for that day. I stood in the doorway over my husband's body just outside the church office followed by an unsettling silence. Thank God for the highly-skilled and dedicated health unit that quickly surrounded him. They had begun resuscitation, and his life was saved. All I could do was pray and will my husband to get up.

That day we experienced God's miracle-working power once again, and I felt a gentle wind blow ever so gently across that wooden floor, breathing life back into my husband's lifeless body. During the ride to the hospital, he talked nonstop, stunning the ambulance driver!

"I shall not die but live, and declare the works of the Lord"- Psalm 118:17

Following his trial sermon that day, my husband was placed on disability but not without a fight; he refused to accept his inability to continue life. His protective nature consumed our conversations, which focused on financial survival and his health. Eventually, he resigned his job in the auto industry and stepped away from preaching. Being the good wife, I respected and supported his heart's desire and request.

Sunday, January 25th, 2015, he returned to the pulpit with the understanding between us that he'd serve only as a guarded spectator. The fiery Baptist preacher's remarks soon turned into a sermon. The congregation froze in fear that he might further harm himself but those fears quickly thawed as we all found ourselves wrapped up in what would become his final sermon.

This brings us to Thursday, February 12, 2015, around 3:00 a.m. where the steaming cup of bitter black tea was served. He intended to sleep quietly away. Eventually, I convinced him to let me anoint his body to help him sleep, which had become our nightly ritual. Around 7:30 p.m. he fell into a deep sleep, and I recall waking up with a shadow standing over me. It was him pointing to the oxygen machine which was pumping away in the corner of the bedroom.

"It's not working; something's wrong!" he said in a panic.

I did my best to reassure and calm him, but he was inconsolable. From there, life went into lighting speed, and 911 was called. The ambulance ride would be his last.

"Mrs. Butler, your husband has not regained consciousness since leaving your home. Should we begin aggravated resuscitation?"
"Really? Aggravated?" I thought.
"No, do not aggravate him." I chose to honor my husband's wishes. "Then come and say your goodbyes."

I found myself standing over my husband's lifeless body, but this time there was a wave of peace over him demanding not to be disturbed. There was nothing left for me to do but drink from that bitter steaming cup. My hardest cry came a few days later after leaving the funeral home planning his Celebration of Life homegoing and realizing he would never put his key in the door lock ever again.

My resilience is wrapped in the hope and belief that for the Christian, death has no lasting sting or victory. For the rest of my life, I must sip from that bitter cup, but the bitterness is tempered with a dash of hope, faith, love, peace, and encouragement in the Word of God. I will see my husband again in that new land he now calls home. My resilience is reinforced with a dash of thankfulness and gratefulness for having the opportunity to live as his wife and partner in ministry. He was ready to go home, and I accepted it.

Do I have moments of unspeakable loneliness? The answer is, YES. Being married to a pastor brings its own set of unique challenges when the pastor suffers fatal illness. What will the wife do? Where will she live? Where will she worship? How will she go forward financially? The greatest challenge for me over the years was discovering ways to help him find balance emotionally, physically, psychologically, socially and spiritually. For each hospital stay, I was afforded the time to be with him, and we never spent a night apart. God alone is my provider, protector, comforter, and guide. I'm certain he prayed a prayer of covering over his family in those final moments. I am blessed to have married one of God's 'anointed and appointed' in the Kingdom.

The freshness of this journey had me feeling like the ugliest fish out of water ordained with an oozing pimple. I soon learned that some just didn't know what to say or were frightened that they just might be next to adorn the title of widow or widower.

If you're reading this, please be kind, loving, and considerate to widows. Know that a smile or hug can make a difference as we move through the grief process. And for the record, don't believe the hype; not all widows are left well-off. For some like me, we must learn how to use tools we never knew how to use. For those on this journey of widowhood, refrain from making major decisions for a short period and absorb the grief. I made regrettable decisions while draped in widow fog. A rework of personal finances is a must and seek assistance because I came very close to folding.

Living abundantly is possible following the death of a spouse. Perhaps you will explore your Chapter Two by dating, remarrying, or finding comfort in becoming a new you. Whatever road you find comfort in, remember your path is as unique as you are. Every day will not be sunny, but the Lord promised to, "never leave us nor forsake us" because "you are fearfully and wonderfully made."

I thank God for the elder widows of the church community who encouraged me on this journey. Thank you for searching my eyes while gaging my progress. Rev. William F. Butler, Jr. fought a good fight, kept the faith and it was time for him to drop his armor, the helmet of salvation, the shield of faith, the belt of truth, the shoes of peace, and lay down his sword.

"The Lord watches over the sojourners; he upholds the widow and the fatherless, but the way of the wicked he brings to ruin." - Psalm 146:9

Chapter 8

The Hustle and Flow of Beverly Kelley-Jeter: The Drink that Remains

Chase died. No. No. That can't be right!

It was a Thursday morning, like any other Thursday morning except it wasn't. That was the last morning that I would leave my husband behind as I went to work, the usual hustle and flow as it were. I had forgotten my wallet that morning; I tend to do these things. My husband, the gallant, chivalrous man that he was, called me and said that he would bring it to me immediately. Well, before I get to the last day of my husband's life, perhaps some backstory is needed. Chase suffered from sarcoidosis. In my husband's case, it was an inflammatory disease which primarily affected his lungs. It had gone into remission for years. However, we did have some health scares, and hospital stays over the years. We were told that although he was having difficulty breathing, it was not sarcoidosis. It was not his lungs nor was it his heart. He was given an inhaler along with tons of other medications and sent on his not-so-merry way, and he was eventually admitted to the hospital for a much longer stay.

The Day He Died

I insisted that I would be ok and that he didn't need to bring my wallet, but he wanted to. I told him to bring it by during lunch because there was a place I wanted to take him. He came by, picked me up, and we enjoyed a nice lunch, although he barely ate any of his salad and did not finish his drink (this was the drink which would remain on my counter for weeks if not months). I could not bear to throw it away. It was the remains of our last meal together, and crazy as that seemed on some level, throwing that drink away would be like throwing a part of him away.

He looked weak. He dropped me off in the parking lot of my job leaving me with the most gentle and loving hug. The kind of hug where you can feel the love filling up your body from your head to your toes. I don't think he said I love you, nor I to him; we just knew. He thanked me for lunch, and he was off.

The Ride to the Hospital

There is nothing that can prepare you for getting THAT phone call from your son or finding the ambulance and the police at your home after you ran every red light to get there. You drive to the hospital not knowing how you actually made it; then I get shuffled to a room while being asked a myriad of questions including if he had heart problems. Noooo... he didn't have heart problems; I was told his heart was fine. Why all these questions? The doctors did all they could, then came the screams. I can still hear my screams, my earth (insert expletive here) scattering screams!

"Would you like to speak to a minister?"

"No."

"Are you sure? Would like to speak to a minister?"

"No." (I'm Agnostic, but at this very moment I'm leaning more towards Atheism)

"What funeral home would you like for us to contact?" they asked.

The nurse, let's call him Nurse Ratchett because I am obliged to hate, took myself and my fourteen-year-old son to see my husband's cold, lifeless body. The man I loved, my best friend, the father of my children, my partner, my lover, was gone. It was all too much to comprehend within a matter of moments. This was a man who was in the hospital a week before, singing in his bed, and making friends. I was not ready for this. I was not ready to let him go. I held his hand, rubbing it as though my love and my warmth could bring him back to life. I was racked with guilt and sorrow. I should have been better; I should have done better. I just kept saying that I was sorry and that I loved him. How did a day that started out so perfectly go so wrong?

Within days of my husband's death, I went to my doctor. I believe that he gave me a prescription for Zoloft. I am not against medication at times like these. However, I had taken this medication before and liked the numbing feeling it gave me. I wanted what I was feeling to be authentic. I needed to feel the gut-wrenching pain, heartbreak, and sorrow.

After the Funeral

Everything seemed blurred. I remember being in bed for days and not being able to sleep in our bed. I remember going to my sister's, sitting on her sofa and falling asleep (I could not lay down to sleep.) My sister's home was my safe place. My youngest spent time with a dear friend and her family. I don't remember where my oldest was. He was twenty-two at the time, and no doubt needed his personal space. It still didn't seem real. I do remember exclaiming," My husband is dead, my husband is dead!" Not only did I mourn his death, but I also mourned a future that would never be. There would be no twenty-fifth wedding anniversary to celebrate; there would be no more proms, high school or college graduations, nor weddings. There would be no more grandchildren or great-grandchildren. There would be no growing old together. The amazingly good-looking man who was my husband now only shared space in my heart.

I See Dead people

I've always felt that my intuition was strong or that I was a little bit psychic. I was sitting at our computer, and I heard my son calling me. When I looked up, there was my husband, not my son. He was healthy and handsome standing there in his boxers, heavier than when he died, with his hairy chest exposed (my son who was 14 was not hairy). I can only describe his face as looking pleasantly peaceful. He was content. I think, or better yet, I know he was telling me that he was fine, he was more than fine; that he was with me. That does not make me miss him any less, but it does bring me peace.

Days later, I dreamed of a lottery number, a Pick 3 to be exact; one of Chase's favorite past-times. Chase would always say that six should be inverted to a nine. Matter of fact, my late brother, (yes, my late brother. Death would visit us again two years later) and he discussed this very thing. The exact number I dreamed of was drawn, but instead of a six, it was a nine. That could only be my Chase.

Do I believe that love transcends death? Yes, with every fiber of my being.

Coping

Medication was not the answer for me. Like I said, I needed to feel everything. If you choose to take prescriptions, by all means, do so. That is between you and your doctor. Everyone takes their own path. No two widows grieve alike or are alike.

I am not much of a talker, except in cases like this. I recognized early on that I needed professional help. I never felt shameful of this fact. Asking for help is a sign of strength, not weakness. I look at it like this - if your leg or any other part of your body was hurting, would you not seek the assistance of a doctor? I needed to unburden on someone; I needed to let it out…my fears, my pain, and at times, insurmountable pain.

I researched grief counselors. I found one who I thought would be perfect for me. She was a black female. She would have to be perfect. It turned out that she was more interested in my timeshare! Next! If the first therapist doesn't fit, don't settle. Your mental health is at stake. Keep searching until you find one that fits. Don't give up.

I eventually found the right fit, and I continue to see her on a regular basis.

I also searched for an online grief support. One of the first being Modern Widow's Club. Back in 2010, there was no other group like this. It was my online safe place. I found a much-needed sense of comradery there. Today, there are many more support groups for widows, including Black Women Widows Empowered.

Besides work, I had to force myself to get out of the house. I needed more than the occasional lunch with friends. It does help to know yourself and how you would best function. I knew that it was not a good idea for me to be secluded. Isolation was not my friend. The internet was. I found Meetup groups there. There were movie groups, girlfriend groups, meditation groups. The most important thing is that I was out and socializing.

Don't underestimate the power of humor. Thank goodness that Chase and I had two amazing sons together who made sure that I laughed hard and often. My husband and I enjoyed countless laughs during the over thirty years that we knew each other. There are times when I have no laughter, but they are now fewer and further apart. My "go to" is Zumba! It's my sanctuary. And, music! I don't think I need to say more.

Okay, so therapy, exercise, music, a sense of humor, and meditation is all well and good, but after over a year of not having the companionship of a male partner, I was consumed with the desire for sex. In a word, I was horny, and the UPS guy was looking really good at this point. (Not to be confused with USPS where my husband worked for over thirty years because that would just be wrong). So yes, sex was my hustle and flow. I did what I needed to do to mask the pain.

I learned new terms like MILF and getting my salad tossed (Google will have to be your friend here). I learned about all things fetish. (Apparently, some men like to be whipped, while some like to be slaves and will even work for members of your family, just tell them what to do and your wish is their command). I'll leave it to your imagination to decide which one I participated in.

There were numerous frivolous sexual encounters, many one-time dates, and a few one night stands. There were a handful of more meaningful relationships and *almost* boyfriends.

And then there was Ryan, (not his real name) who I will only speak of with love. This was a relationship that would last for over five years. In many cases, he felt like my lifesaver. He was my confidant on many occasions; he was the man I could turn to, the one who would say everything will be okay, he was the one that told me that I was beautiful (and I believed him). He was the first man to tell me he loved me since my husband had died. He was my much younger lover; my friend with "benefits".

My Brother was Murdered

I was two years in, and I was still grieving, but I was at the point where no one at work would notice. I was holding it together pretty well, or so I thought. I was at the point where I was in real trouble; I wasn't getting work done according to the agency's standards. Heck, my youngest son and I had just gotten back from our first big vacation since Chase had passed. It was the trip to Hawaii that Chase and I had talked about taking for our 25th wedding anniversary, the one we never saw. We were going to take the boys with us. It was one of the best vacations ever. I could see the proverbial light at the end of the stinking tunnel. We were going to be okay. That feeling was short-lived, and my high was downgraded to the lowest of all lows when my sister told me that my brother had been murdered. And so the cycle began again. Grief isn't something you can prepare for. The guilt hits. Although I was hundreds of miles away, I thought to myself how I had spoken highly about him the night he was killed. Why didn't I call him? If I had called, maybe something in the 'continuum time thingy' would have changed. Maybe, with all of these magical powers that I have, I could have saved him. Ridiculous, right? My head knew that, but my heart would never accept it. The guilt remains with me regarding my husband's death, too. I should have made him eat better. I should have cooked more. I should have loved him better, and thus the need for continued therapy I suppose.

Another Significant Loss

In April 2016 my dear friend was admitted to the hospital, very ill but aware of her surroundings. She decided that she wanted me to become her Power of Attorney. I was now responsible for her financial decisions and with the medical directive, I became responsible regarding her health issues.

On that first day that I saw Cathy, (not her real name) I had no idea that things would go from bad to worse. Cathy had a massive stroke and was no longer able to communicate verbally. She was able to communicate by nodding her head, and I consulted her regarding lifesaving measures. I consulted her until she was discharged from the nursing home and sent to the hospital. A decision had to be made. It was time to say goodbye to my friend. The friend who had reached out to me when Chase died. She had been present. She showed up. This was the absolute hardest decision I ever made, but I knew it was the right one.

My grief compounded. I became functionally depressed, but I had to get things done. I had more responsibilities then I had before when it came to this horrid stuff. Every bill I looked at brought me back to Chase's death to the point where I had to take a break from it; yes I took a break from the paperwork and from people who made my life more difficult at the time. I had the right. You have the right. No is a complete sentence. Things that did not have to get done did not. My only obligation was to Cathy at this time.

I was told that grief could affect you physically. It can. It did. It is important to take care of your physical health as well as your mental health. Keep those doctor and dentist appointments. Take care of you.

I have learned that grief is not something that you can go around or ignore in the hope that it will go away. Grief is something that you must go through. There is no given length of time to grieve, and it does not happen in an orderly or step-by-step fashion. Take it day by day, hour by hour, and minute by minute if you must. This is not something that you have to go through alone. Please reach out for help.

You will never be the same. You will change. You have changed. There is hope. There is that stinking light at the end of the proverbial tunnel (or something like that). The heart is resilient, no matter how much pain others may inflict upon it, it will always stand the test of time, it will always grow stronger and will proudly say; I am resilient, not insensitive.

Chapter 9

The Hustle and Flow of Angela Richardson Allen: My Destiny into Dating Continues

Peace I leave with you, my peace I give unto you: not as the world giveth, give I unto you. Let not your heart be troubled, neither let it be afraid.

John 14:27

My Plans Changed

Most girls dream of being married and living happily ever after. I had my fairytale wedding, exotic honeymoon, and home. Our family started within six months of being married; I became pregnant with our daughter. Three years ago, I lost my husband to what I describe as a premature death and my happily ever after ended when my spouse didn't wake up on Mother's Day. If time could stop, my life as I knew it changed overnight, time stopped for three full days as I laid on the bed in disbelief and wondering when the reoccurring dream would stop. When I was growing up widows were older women in their sixties and seventies, not their thirties and forties. I was being initiated into the club of widows. My membership was confirmed and sealed, not to be revoked. When faced with the darkness of loss, it's difficult to see the light of anything possible, beautiful, or good on the other side of the pain and despair. What's good about my daughter growing up without her father, without him seeing her off to the prom and walking her down the aisle in marriage? Diamonds are formed from coal under high pressure and temperature, with the pressure of loss we will become different but greater because of what we went through.

On my road to face grief and loss, I was determined to get healing and find tools to help my family grow. I attended a peer grief counseling group that offered lots of statistical data and feedback from other widows and widowers of what one can expect after the loss of a spouse. In one session, the leader warned the widows and widowers not to be surprised if they stopped being invited to couples' events or for the women not to be surprised if they now become a threat to women whose husbands offer to help with projects around the home. Without realizing it, people may begin to separate from you. The very thought of widows offers the realization that death is real I leaned on my family and great friends who were amazingly supportive in offering a listening ear or whatever I needed. This support allowed me to accept that I was not left alone to figure things out for myself but that God has people who will remind you of His love and concern toward us.

When I married my spouse, we were best friends. We talked about retirement and growing older together rocking on a swing on the porch and watching our grandchildren play while sipping southern sweet tea. I was with my spouse ten years and together two years beforehand. As far as dating, it took some time to open up to the idea of dating another man. I never thought of dating or becoming involved with anyone. Dating required time and commitment. I was not willing to share my time away from my daughter. On the contrary, I began to feel like a black widow spider with a widow sign plastered on my forehead and simultaneously desiring to be invisible. Praying to God to please keep anyone from approaching me. I purposefully joined an all-white church to help me disappear. Some would ask the question within weeks of his death, "Do you think you will get married again?" I realized early on that type of questioning was called rushed grief. Although their intentions are good, some people won't understand what to say. While grieving, there are feelings of vulnerability. Protect your grief process and be strong enough to tell others they are intrusive and that's not a subject you are willing to discuss.

Grieving on Purpose

As time passed, I took every opportunity to remain healthy in my grief process. My dear friend stated that I was healthy before so it was imperative that I grieve rationally and healthily. My daughter and I both attended peer grief classes, clinical counseling, and Christian counseling. Dating was nowhere near my radar; rather I hustled to create the new normal for my daughter and me. The loss of a spouse also creates voids in what that spouse contributed to the home. In my case my spouse left voids in the areas of finances, assistance with transportation, raising our child from a father's love and companionship. So, it is with any void you work to fill it, relieve it or replace it.

Fear became my companion in some ways. One of the greatest challenges I faced was understanding to relinquish control of things I could not control. My spouse dying in his sleep presented another real fear I fought to overcome. My sleep pattern was terrible. I fought to stay awake because I allowed my mind to whisper to me that I wouldn't wake up. While grieving, I invited so many other anxieties into my life. After several sessions with a Counselor, she shared a few powerful points. The first was that death was out of my control. The second was for me to create a routine for sleeping as I did for my daughter. I put this into practice and soon fear no longer kept me awake.

The Head, Not the Tail

When the loss of a spouse occurs, there are also physical and tangible losses to accompany the process. My spouse was the breadwinner of our family. His death deleted his income from our household. The thought of managing things on my own caused doubt in myself. When I was grieving, I lost a bit of esteem and self-confidence. I didn't feel comfortable making immediate decisions that would affect our future. Time passes so fast that it's important to set goals, create a budget and ask the hard questions. How long will the life insurance last? Can I manage this home with one income? Can my daughter continue to participate in extracurricular sports? How long do I have to make a final decision? Will I need to move and downsize? Can I afford the COBRA Health Insurance premium?

The inner turmoil I felt as I became the head of household was daunting and shaped a lot of anxiety which ultimately bred fear. As a businesswoman, one of my companies is a Sports and Marketing Event Planning boutique. Our goal is to plan events for high-profile professional athletes, sporting events and celebrity fundraisers. I have a plan for everything and a contingency plan for when things don't go as planned, so there's about a 6% room for error. But God doesn't promise life will not present trails and heartache. I needed his peace each minute as the worrying racing thoughts of tomorrow clouded my mind.

Unexpectedly, one day it was as if another level of energy empowered me. I felt a God-confidence to begin to plan the steps necessary for creating a stable environment for my daughter and me. The first thing I did was to secure a Business and Life Coach, which is available free for Veteran wives. We began to process through my plan for expanding my business and created manageable small steps. Once I accomplished a step, I celebrated. Little by little I became more creative and excited about all the possibilities. With that excitement and a manageable plan, I decided I was confident to be able to take care of my family.

Overcoming fear means turning fear into power. Even when you face a real problem or danger, the Holy Spirit's discernment can transform that fear warning into urgency and energy, fueling you to act instead of freezing up. With this fuel of the Holy Spirit, I successfully created additional income streams as my goal towards my desired goal. The goal I created would maintain the current lifestyle we were accustomed to living. With strength and determination, I worked tirelessly on my businesses to become profitable.

My Heart Responded

Time passes so quickly and some days seem to run together, but at the end of the day, the realization of loneliness creeps in. I developed a business; I worked, did charity work and went to church. My daughter and I created Friday night family night. We watched a movie in our home theater, ate pizza and dessert. Depending on the weather we sometimes went for a walk. I knew it was important that I not create an unhealthy relationship with my daughter where she was my constant companion. She was my daughter and the lines needed to remain clear. She wasn't there to replace my spouse. We had a great mother-daughter bond that I purposely continued to nurture. In times of loneliness, I would call my mother sometimes in tears and angered that I was left alone without companionship and she'd encourage me saying, "Its ok baby, God has someone for you, you're still young, you'll marry again don't close your heart."

I recall an interesting experience from peer counseling. The mailman delivers a first wedding invitation; they dreaded the thought of seeing someone say their vows, kiss, have their first dance. It was like a grief trigger. While you are happy for the couple, there was sadness that you attend the wedding alone and you may cry the entire time for your loss as they hear the pastor recite, "Til death do you part." The tears shed is not because you are happy for the couple but because of the personal experience of loss. A sense of envy can cause you to feel false emotions towards the couple when you are genuinely happy for them.

Most of my friends who knew and loved my spouse and I as a couple thought I should date. Some recommended dating sites. Some wanted to introduce me to their single handsome and successful friend, business associate or relative. They would bring a resume of their accomplishments, family history, dating or marital history. I remember one friend sending me a picture of his friend because I was 'too sweet to be alone.' I withdrew myself because I am not the average woman. I had never been on a blind date nor was I willing to be. I wanted to take careful consideration in dating because I had a young daughter. I had to protect her from my choices.

I spoke earlier about relieving pain; I could not date just because I yearned to relieve the pain of loneliness. It was important for me to trust God to send my mate while keeping my feelings in perspective. And that was my prayer: *God, prepare my heart to know the man you are sending into my life that will be my husband and to prepare my heart to open enough to love again. The heart in its capacity is deep and endless. God protect me from any person who doesn't have good intentions for me or my daughter. God order my steps.*

Nearly three years later, while living a content life, working hard in my businesses and not thinking of dating, I had an encounter. I visited a possible new client who needed my services. A mutual friend referred him. When I walked by the client, I felt a tickle within myself. I was shocked that I had that response. But the response was internal, a spiritual knowledge that comes from God. It was in that instant I prayed for guidance and direction for what followed.

The client escorted me to a seat. After sitting down with the client and exchanging general pleasantries, we began to a conversation. The conversation was without pretense. The conversation covered a generation of topics in those moments. I didn't expect anything except to speak from my heart. We exchanged as if we'd been lifelong friends. He caused me to laugh from my gut; you know the one where you are bent over holding your stomach. He asked me if we could pray, so we did. He asked if I trusted him, without reluctance. I said *yes,* and we danced with no music. Our conversation lasted nearly three hours. No part of the engaging conversation was about business, but it naturally flowed. The afternoon conversation turned into an evening movie and more conversation. We spent nearly ten hours together the first day. The connection was indescribable and refreshing. There was almost a sense of guilt trying to seep into my mind, but I immediately took control of that thought. I know that dating and remarriage is a choice, so I decided in my heart that I was open for both.

My heart responded and opened because I realized I still had room to love again. I love the covenant of marriage. I loved being married. The capacity of the heart is immensely dense and wide. Love is a choice to receive and to freely give. Feelings are fleeting and temporary but can be gone in an instant. In the grief cycle, it's typical to feel several emotions simultaneously. In the Bible, love is described so delicately. Love is patient, kind, and is not proud. It is everlasting and continuous. As my heart beats, that's an indication I am still alive. God has given me breath, and I want to embrace every ounce of love that He has destined I receive. I loved being in love, loving my spouse and others and receiving love. Because I choose to open my heart for new love doesn't denote I have forgotten the imprints left in my heart by my spouse, on the contrary, it describes my desire to continue to live and be in the present, in my NOW and planting seeds in my future.

There is beauty being formed in the journey of pain and darkness. With grief and loss, there is no perfect equation to how one ought to grieve. The pain and darkness of loss breeds fear and is far-reaching and can immobilize us into unhealthy behaviors like depression, over-indulgences, addictions, and isolation. Fear is an enemy to God because fear causes you to doubt not just yourself, but what God can do for you. At the same time, fear is a familiar companion; a false friend that enables you to remain stuck, not moving forward or growing. Having positive momentum in the grief journey was essential for me to move to a place to receive from the future, instead of constantly grieving what will never be again. I will never be married to my first spouse again. He will never touch me again. He will never speak to me again. He will never hold me. He is gone from this life and resting with God. Make the decision today to live in the present. Living in the present will lead to greater blessings in the future.

This collaborative book with these amazingly brave and courageous authors is an indication that our hearts are transparent so that we can help someone in their grief journey to continue to live life to the fullest. Life is for the living, LIVE, LIVE, LIVE!

Chapter 10

The Hustle and Flow of Melody Dixon-Brown: Journaling My Despair of Mental Health and Self-Therapy

On January 27, 2014, my husband, Anthony, died unexpectedly of a massive heart attack. I moved forward without him, teaching at The University of North Carolina at Charlotte, raising my teenaged sons – Richard and Robert, and taking care of my ailing mother. One of the ways I've coped with the loss of my husband is to keep a journal and express my feelings, frustrations, and joys in writing. Here are some excerpts from my journal since Anthony passed away. This personal journal helped keep me sane over the past few years, and I hope you can relate to my journey as a widow while finding some hope and solace in my writing.

My "hustle and flow" is based on resilience and a self-awareness of my feelings of grief and how to cope.

Monday, January 27, 2014

When I woke up this morning at 5:45 a.m., I didn't think or even imagine that I would go to bed a widow. My beloved husband, Anthony, died at 7:01 a.m. He was going about his routine, preparing for work. He had a massive heart attack and collapsed on the stairs.

The medics worked on him for 20 minutes but couldn't save him. I have this morning etched in my memory, including the way Anthony looked as he gasped for air and tried desperately to remain in this world.

My life changed in an instant. My heart aches.

Sunday, March 23, 2014

"Though nothing can bring back the hour of splendor in the grass, or glory in the flower, we will grieve not, rather find strength in what remains behind..." *Ode – Intimations of Immortality from Recollections of Early Childhood* - William Wordsworth (1770-1850).

I miss Anthony every day. I am trying to find strength in what remains – my children. Although Richard and Robert are just becoming men, I still cling to them for my strength and happiness. I know I'll have to let go and "get a life" of my own – without Anthony. That's the hard part.

Mother's Day – May 11, 2014

It's a beautiful sunny day. Robert made mom and I breakfast, and we'll have dinner together this evening at Red Lobster.

I'm feeling pretty good. The semester ended well (teaching two large lecture classes) and I now have some much-needed time off.

I'm taking Robert to his job at McDonald's this morning. I'm grateful that he's finally earning his keep (smile). That's why he can afford a nice Mother's Day gift for me ($25 gift card to Bath & Body Works).

This is my first Mother's Day without Anthony. I'm handling it ok, but I think Father's Day will be tough. We're going to visit Anthony's grave (me, Rich, and Rob).

At this point, I need to keep my two main goals in front of me and prepare for the summer:

1. Goal 1 – Stay healthy. I'm my son's only living parent.

2. Goal 2 – Save money. I've got to recover from the financial loss of my husband.

Thursday, May 27, 2014

It's a beautiful sunny 67-degree morning. I woke up, took Robert to school, and then fixed mom cereal and went walking for an hour and a half.

My walks always clear my head and let me think out loud while inhaling fresh air and enjoying God's nature.

Today's walk cleared my head and gave me a little energy. Lord knows I needed some energy. I'm tired! I'm tired of being responsible for this house – all the repairs, ongoing maintenance, lawn care, etc. Also, I'm still financially responsible for my almost adult children and my mom. I don't see myself retiring anytime soon.

As for mom, I love her dearly, but I've been her primary caregiver for ten years, and her dementia continues to get worse. It's exhausting emotionally and physically. I pray to God to give me the strength to continue to take care of her. This experience has also motivated me to contribute to long-term care insurance so my children won't worry about taking care of me. Although I would never put my mom in a nursing home, I'm okay with my children putting me in one (especially if I have dementia or Alzheimer's).

I don't think anyone ever expects to be sandwiched in between their kids and their parents, but that responsibility is very real for me. I just wish Anthony was here to help me shoulder it.

Thursday, June 5, 2014

I MUST SELL THIS HOUSE! The financial burden, maintenance, and repairs are overwhelming:

1. Mortgage + Equity Loan + Utilities + Homeowners Fee + Maintenance Costs = UNSUSTAINABLE EXPENSES

2. I prefer to be a RENTER than an OWNER. I'm tired of the responsibility of a house.

3. I need to investigate the cost to rent vs. own...perhaps a condo or a townhouse.

I've got to get the house cleaned and ready to sell it next year possibly. I know there are a lot of repairs to make – painting, re-tiling the bathroom, redoing the hardwood floors, and installing new carpet. I'd also like to relandscape the lawn and cut down some of the trees overlooking the house (trees that attract squirrels and threaten the house during bad storms).

I don't know where I'm going to get the money or time to make these changes, but I MUST SELL THIS HOUSE!

Monday, June 30, 2014

Yesterday, I found myself in a deep depression. Today, I'm brushing myself off and reflecting on all of my blessings. I know I can't always shake off my depression, and I've talked to my grief counselor about this many times. However, I've found the best way to dig myself out of depression is to stop and THANK GOD for all he has done for me.

First, I thank God for a wonderful summer thus far. I took time to enjoy a wonderful vacation, concerts, and festivals, and lunches with several dear friends. Despite money being tight, I've managed my debts very well and take advantage of every coupon and "freebie" I can get. God knows I've worked very hard to earn what I have (and am still working this summer).

Second, I am blessed with two wonderful sons. I wish I could spend more time with them, but Richard goes back to West Point after two weeks home. He leaves today. Robert will be traveling with AAU basketball over the next four weeks, and I will get a taste of what life will be like next fall (2015) when I am home with mom and am truly an "empty nester."

My goals now are to sell the house (but try to refinance before I sell it), prepare for second summer session (which starts this Tuesday), prepare for the fall (new online course), and learn to adapt to a life that doesn't revolve around my children.

Selling the house and getting rid of all these memories is pivotal to starting my new life. It's the start of me overcoming the depression and anxiety I feel in leaving my old life.

Tuesday, July 8, 2014

I usually set goals and often achieve them. Today, I'm claiming some key goals for next year and look forward to these changes in my life and my family:

1. Help Robert get into college. He will be preparing for fall semester classes this time next year.

2. Sell this house! I'll be living in a low-maintenance, easy-to-clean, 1700 square foot condo or townhouse in a nice, secure neighborhood.

3. Invest in long-term care insurance and a Roth IRA.

Sunday, July 13, 2014

It's 10:33 a.m. on a Sunday. I woke up, put mom in the shower, made breakfast, and lazily got ready to go to the movies with a friend (Dawn of the Planet of the Apes).

Rob is at an AAU tournament, Rich is at West Point's Camp Buckner (going through a grueling basic training), and I'm getting a taste of what life will be like when I'm an "empty nester." It's clear that I must "get a life" and keep busy by socializing, volunteering, and doing for others.

I must get myself motivated to take better care of my health and find fulfilling activities to fill my days once the boys (or rather men) are no longer at home.

Wednesday, August 8, 2014

Random thoughts...

Good day – good week thus far (first week of classes). The week started off a bit chaotic, but I'm off to a good start. Lots of work left to do (complete online course quizzes and grade books for all four classes). Overall, I think this will be the BEST semester I've ever had. If not for Anthony's passing, last spring semester would've been great too. I'm looking forward to the challenge of online teaching as well as a new crop of students to work with.

The only negative this week is my finances. I've just checked my budget for the month. I've blown my food budget by almost $200 thanks to hosting family/guests for a week. I love my family, but I hate the bill that comes after every visit.

Robert's first week of high school (his senior year) went very well. He's at a new charter school where Anthony coached basketball. The teachers, coaches, and staff are wonderful! They've welcomed us like family and continue to honor Anthony's memory. I'm getting used to carpooling again...and I still hate it.

Tuesday, January 6, 2015

It has almost been one year since Anthony passed. I cried yesterday because I hated starting the New Year without him.

However, I must move on with my life. I've begun to think about what I want my life to be like over the next 15 years until retirement. Here is the vision I have for myself:

- GREAT health - 150 lbs. or less – normal blood pressure and blood sugar; no psoriasis
- Stress-free! - Meditate, pray, exercise, practice yoga – do whatever it takes to manage stress
- Drive a Prius – I'm tired of paying these high gas prices!
- Exercise regularly – look good and feel good
- Travel frequently - weekend trips and week-long trips
- Eat out often – stop pretending that I love to cook when I know damn well I hate it
- Socialize often with 50+ set
- Read! - at least one book a week
- Relax – savor my peace and quiet
- Visit family often
- Volunteer in schools and library
- SAVOR every moment of my life and work; don't wait until retirement to enjoy life

Thursday, March 19, 2015

Well, I just reviewed my short-term goals for 2015-2016. I have to laugh because I have changed or deleted most of those goals from the list. A lot has changed since my last entry two months ago.

First, I realize that my vision of selling the house and living maintenance-free as an apartment renter is a joke. Seriously, I was stuck in the 80's in terms of rental costs. Here I was thinking that I could rent a one-bedroom apartment/condo in Charlotte, North Carolina in a decent part of town, with amenities such as a washer/dryer, fitness center, and walking trails for $800/month with utilities for $200 or less. I got the wake-up call of my life when I started researching nearby apartments and condos. The rents for a one-bedroom apartment were higher than my re-financed mortgage for a five-bedroom house. Also, the rents can go up as much as 10% each year! What happened to the good old days where people rented for life, and the rent increases were minimal? Last but not least, when I researched townhouses and patio-style condos in my area, I learned that the mortgage would be higher (and a high monthly maintenance/homeowner's fee) for less space. Bottom line…I would be spending a lot of money to sell my house for a home where I paid more per month for less space. It is far wiser for me to stay here and invest in repairing and maintaining this house rather than move to an apartment or buy a new home. What the hell was I thinking?

As for my low gas mileage Prius, I'll have to pay off my current car and ride it until it falls apart. I'm done with car payments. If I do buy another car, it will be with cash.

As for the frequent travel and restaurant meals, I'll have to get real about those goals as well. I'm going to be on a tight budget for many years. I'm okay with it, as long as I can "treat myself" now and then. God is good.

Monday, May 4, 2015

Today was a good day. I finished my classes (Event Planning, Language Craft) and hope to put grades in tomorrow. The weather was very beautiful (sunny, 80 degrees), and I'm looking forward to Robert's graduation on June 4th.

Finally, I was reappointed to my senior lecturer position (five-year contract) until May 15, 2020. I plan to leave teaching at the age of 59. I'm thinking about advising or career counseling at UNC Charlotte OR working as a nanny or daycare worker. As much as I love teaching, I'm beginning to burn out. I'm ready for a "new adventure" in my career. ☺

Monday, May 11, 2015

Free at last! The spring 2015 semester is over!! I just turned in my grades for the semester and put on my email autoreply. I have the entire summer off! I haven't had that luxury (a big benefit of academia) for over five years! ☺

So...today will be a day of reflection and renewal.

Reflection

I remember end-of-spring semesters when the boys were young. I looked forward to assisting with class parties and special events, elementary and middle school graduations, and "field days" where the boys competed in fun games like the balloon toss with fellow students.

I remember buying educational booklets and playing board games with the boys. I remember planning weekly summer schedules of "Mommy Camp" – reading, writing, and math in the morning – library visits, museums, Carowinds amusement park in the afternoons.

I remember family summer vacations to Florida and Hilton Head. I remember. Most of all, I remember a time with my wonderful husband. Sure. Things weren't always sweet. We argued, fussed, and fought, but we always made up.

Renewal

Although I remember and savor my past, I truly am looking forward to my future. I am going through a process of renewal:

- Renewing my health by eliminating processed foods, high-carb meals, soda, sugar, salt, and fat from my diet
- Renewing my health by exercising more (not just walking) – yoga, Zumba

- Renewing my faith by reading the Bible, especially the New Testament and passages where Jesus spoke to us directly
- Renewing my peace of mind by meditating (scripture, Deepak Chopra)
- Renewing my relationship with my mother by learning to be more thankful for her despite the challenges of caring for her
- Renewing my relationship with my sons by being more patient and understanding with them – by listening more and giving unsolicited advice less
- Renewing my relationship with other members of my family by spending more time with them and saying "No" more often and being indirect and passive less
- Renewing my relationship with my friends by smiling and laughing more, vacationing with them, and complaining/venting less
- Renewing my financial health by budgeting, saving, and investing more – in denying myself (less eating out, less buying new clothes, no manicures/pedicures, etc.) but splurging now and then.

Tuesday, June 7. 2016

It has been over a year since I wrote in this journal. It may be because I'm feeling good – healthy, strong, and focused. I've seen my grief counselor a few times, but I find more solace in talking to my network of widows and close friends and family.

Also, I've already checked off some of my summer "to do" list items – create a will, invest in a Roth IRA, maintain my house with upgrades to my bathroom and new appliances in my kitchen. I've also begun to de-clutter the house and work on my fall courses.

Most importantly, I'm eating right and exercising regularly.

Proud of myself. Life is good. ☺

Saturday, June 18, 2016

I took a walk this morning instead of going to Zumba class. I needed to clear my mind and inhale fresh air. It was a rough morning that started with mom wetting the bed.

I took Rob to work at Jack-in-the-Box (he has another part-time job later this afternoon at Harris Teeter), and I now plan to focus on redesigning my courses and decluttering and cleaning the house.

I must admit that I've been a bit lazy during this first month of summer vacation. I realize that I must prepare for fall and start to get motivated about teaching again. I also have to maintain this house.

I'm trying my best to hold it all together, but there are days when I think my sanity is hanging by a thread. I miss Anthony so much (tomorrow is Father's Day), but I realize that I've got to "hold it down" for the sake of my boys.

Finally, I realize that pain, suffering, and death are a part of life that we cannot escape. All we can do is carry on and call on God for our strength and mercy.

Tuesday, September 6, 2016

Yesterday, September 5, was not only Labor Day, but it was my 29th wedding anniversary. I miss Anthony every day. I wonder how life would be if he were still here.

In any case, I'M STILL HERE! As I conclude this two-year journal of my life, I reflect on all the joys, tragedies, and anxieties that I experienced. God has given me the strength to keep going.

I'm not sure what life has in store for me, but I plan to keep going by strengthening my faith and relationship with God. I hope he will continue to bless me with physical, mental, emotional, and spiritual strength. I hope he will give me PEACE and a stress-free life. I hope he will give me financial security and peace of mind knowing that my bills are paid, and I have no debts.

Finally, I pray God will bless my children – Richard and Robert. I pray for their happiness, peace of mind, physical, emotional, and spiritual strength. I hope they marry beautiful, smart women who love and respect them (and give me plenty of grandchildren).

My faith is strong, and I believe.

Sunday, September 11, 2016

Yesterday would have been Anthony's 56th birthday, and today is the 15th anniversary of the terrorist attack on the World Trade Center and the Pentagon.

I am reminded of how fleeting and precious life is. This journey called life is not limitless. It will end—at any time. Tomorrow is NOT promised.

I'm trying to SAVOR each day while planning for tomorrow. I'm truly at a crossroads in my life. I have lost my passion for teaching and have a desire to change my career focus once again. Also, I'm struggling as a caregiver for mom. Her dementia is getting progressively worse, she's going blind, and the strain of caring for her is affecting my health (and mental well-being).

I must make a change…not sure what that change will be, or when…but a change is coming. That change may be a move away from Charlotte to another state. I can sell the house, which is what I originally planned two years ago, and start fresh somewhere else.

All I know is a change is coming, and I'm so ready for it!

Friday, September 16, 2016

"Ahimsa" …this is a Sanskrit word I used in yoga this week. It means:

"Compassion"

"Do no harm" to any living thing, and

"Non-violent response."

Ahimsa comes from one of the eight pillars of yoga. It requires discipline in your response to others. No matter how much you disagree or dislike the other person, you must show restraint and "do no harm" in your response. Recognize the other person as a precious being on this earth and respect them. It also means forgiving and respecting oneself – showing oneself forgiveness, compassion, and non-violence.

I struggle with this when dealing with my anger and natural tendencies to argue, fight, and do emotional "violence" with others' feelings (especially those I love).

Also, worrying is considered to be a form of violence according to the concept of Ahimsa. When you worry, you send the message to the other persons that you don't trust them, that their choices aren't good ones. How many times have I conveyed "worry" and "concern" to Robert thinking that he perceived my worry as "caring" and "love." All he perceived was that I didn't trust his choices, and I wanted to control him.

I'm going to keep working on "Ahimsa," but I have a long way to go in applying that doctrine in my own life – to others and to myself.

Monday, October 10, 2016

I have a pit in my stomach. It's one of those stomach knots or pits that comes from anxiety.

The anxiety comes from the fact that I am overwhelmed and my free time (which I need plenty of) is not my own. This past month, I gained another class, agreed to do a department workshop, and watched my mother go completely blind and helpless.

They say God doesn't put more on you than you can handle. I'm not sure, and I have a pit in my stomach to prove it.

Saturday, October 29, 2016

Epiphany! Feeling "spiritual" today and had an epiphany…

There is a direct correlation between being a "child of God" and being a parent. There is dual perspective here that I never recognized before.

I get very frustrated, angry and disappointed with my children when they are disrespectful, disobedient, and ungrateful. When I consider all I do for my children, it makes me sad that they do not appreciate it. The more I do, the more I raise expectations that I will do more.

I now realize that I behave the same ways as a "child of God." I get angry and resentful when God doesn't give me what I want. The more He blesses me, the more blessings I expect. When I face troubles, and things don't go my way, I get mad at God. At times, I am ungrateful, disrespectful, and disobedient in carrying out God's word.

So…my epiphany leads me to challenge myself to do the following daily:

1. Be grateful! Savor each day and each blessing – no matter what troubles or hardships I'm having that day.
2. Be patient! I need to be patient and loving with my own children when they are disobedient and disrespectful because God is patient with me as His disobedient child.
3. Be obedient to God! Read his Word carefully and do as He commands.

This has been a long and difficult journey as a widow and caregiver. However, I know that God loves me, and like any good parent will always be there for me.

My journal has been a form of self-therapy in coping with grief and other stresses of life. I encourage other widows to "journal their despair" and express yourselves in writing.

Chapter 11

The Hustle and Flow of Maureen Bobo: My Dance with Grief

When I think of the term, *Hustle and Flow,* as it relates to my journey as a widow -- I view it as a dance. You can't dance without music. Therefore, I've chosen songs that speak of various stages in my life to relay my story. Some of these songs are relatively new, and some are not so new, but my selections aren't about my favorite songs. The music and lyrics remind me of destinations, both physical and emotional, that I have visited in the past seven years as a widow.

My husband, Martin Quinn Bobo, suffered from chronic heart disease. His death has affected my life in a way nothing else has. Maybe that's why I felt so alone and isolated.

Where do I, a girl interrupted, go from here?

Martin and I were married for thirteen years and together for seventeen. Time doesn't stand still. But, wouldn't it have been wonderful if me and two my daughters, ages eight and two months at the time of Martin's death, were able to grieve without interruption and return to the world when we were finished?

Of course, life doesn't work that way, and when I figured that out, I thought, *now what?*

Grief doesn't work that way, either. You must go *through* it, and *lean into* the pain. In that space and time, I believed that I had to make a decision: would I live in that place of despair forever and never moving forward? Or would I take a chance and step out from my grief?

I had to create my own path: be a pioneer, and dance to the music of my survival.

***

On the day of Martin's funeral, as I stood before his coffin, I continually reminded myself that, *to be absent from the body you are present with the Lord.* I told myself, "You have to remind yourself of what you heard in your upbringing," Thank God I listened during church services. Still, I questioned Him. "Lord, why? Lord, how?"

So, there I was with my 8-year-old child, Jordan and holding my two-month-old, Mikayla in my arms. I couldn't believe it was happening. The funeral attendant motioned for me to cover Martin with the shroud. I did, and I placed his Bible in the coffin.

Have you ever had an out-of-body experience where you felt as if you were watching yourself from a corner? That's how I felt on that day, and it had happened to me twice before. The first was in 1997 when my mother had uterine cancer surgery and passed away three months later. The second instance was when I lost my son, Micah, in the hospital. He came too soon. At just eighteen weeks gestation the doctors told me that the earliest a baby could survive was at 22 weeks gestation. They listened to his heartbeat all day until it stopped. There I was in that corner crouching, watching myself crying an ocean as I gave birth to my son who was already in the afterlife. They put him in a little basket and fortunately, I was able to be with him all night. Alone in that hospital room, I bounced him on my knee (the way my mother used to do when I was little), which led the way for the preparation of my life walk – the widow's walk. Nothing can prepare you for death, for grief. It's a dance - a hustle and flow; two steps forward, three steps back. A dance needs music, and that's what I'm attempting to accomplish throughout my story. I now believe that I am qualified to address my former self with this commentary of my journey.

Back to the coffin...

I gathered my emotions. "You got 'dis girl," I whispered to myself before allowing them to close the coffin.

"Is the baby ok?" I pondered.

I looked around. "Jordan, where are you?" I probed.

My daughter's entire second-grade class attended the funeral and thank God she was interacting with them.

"Mommy, why does daddy have on makeup?" she asked.

I had no words. I just knew that I had a difficult task of dancing with Grief.

One, two, three-step. One, two, three-step. Make sure it's right! One, two, three-step!

I glanced up. Grief lingered for me. I walked towards him. He nodded, motioned towards the exit and held out its hand. We left together.

F.R.F.R (For Real, For Real)

Martin's sudden death knocked my world off its axis. I was left alone to raise two children. I was angry at people, the world, and God -- mostly God. Yes, I'm a Christian. Yes, I had every right to be angry. My kids were suffering, and *my black kids ain't have no black daddy!* (Yes, I said it in ebonics).

Grief led me to where no one wanted to tread: a place where it was in control, and I was not. Grief leads to where no one wants to tread. Grief carried me way up to the heavens and threw me to the ground, crushing my spirit like a grape, and stood on my neck and laughed at me when I cried. He's a mean partner – where the more you try to get away, the more you feel his presence.

You want to die, but death won't come. It's the psychedelic emotional dance floor. *Grief's Disco*, I guess. You're just a rag doll as he plays with you, the children and my finances. I'm all alone! No one will ever love me, I repeated to myself. Everybody hates me!

Grief will grin his wicked, toothless grin and whispers in your ear during the slow dance and you scream and hold on to the hope of tomorrow.

I pushed back and gave him a challenge. I was alone. Grief was leading the dance, for real.

Ain't nothing lonelier than a lonely widow.

I was feeling isolated.

I still want to be held.

Not every man can handle a widow's heart. Seven years have passed. And now here I stand, still grieving alone. But. I'm alone with purpose.

I want companionship. I'll just be totally honest. I want sex! But I follow Christ, and I am doing my widowed life God's way. That's another book, my sistahs.

My Dance. My Hustle. My Flow

While Grief is twirling you around the dance floor of your circumstances, you scream and hold on to the hope for tomorrow. As a Christian, I had an anchor, Christ, who kept me from drowning at the height of my sorrow. Eventually, I'd get my chance to lead this dance. I just had to bide my time. I slept, ate, and prayed – not to wake up but not to die either. What's the difference? My judgment was clouded.

My advice for the grieving widow is this: never make major decisions for at least two years after the death of a loved one. During that time, Grief is most likely piloting your course. As time went on, I gained strength. The abuse made me stronger. Grief tried to kill me, but God was building me. I began to dwell on the song, "Take Me to the King," by Tamela Mann.

My hustle as a widow began to flow. I co-authored a book with two other women called, *The Unwelcome Committee*. It's the story of the journey of three young widows navigating through grief. I also went a step further and contributed my story to the anthology, *Grief Diaries: Poetry, Prose and More*, which offers expressive and artistic writings about grief.

The Processing Plant

Loneliness escorted me to what I called, "God's Processing Plant." I had to go. I needed work. God had a plan and purpose for me. He has one for you, too. If loneliness doesn't take you under, grief will. Be aware of his tactics!

In the Processing Plant, God takes control. It won't feel good, but you start to realize there is a method to the madness. God must prepare you for your purpose. I agree with that, but as time went on. I started to get a little stronger because although Grief was abusive to me, the abuse was making me stronger. God was beginning to build me. Grief's grasp became a little looser as I upgraded my rag doll status to something that was growing a backbone. He shockingly looked at me and grinned. Did I see the fear in his eyes? Didn't matter because I was enduring my hustle, my flow…so that I could dance.

I was *down* in the Processing Plant, not *out*. I spent my time there growing in the Lord and getting closer to Christ. I didn't feel controlled by Grief as much. His time was limited in leading the dance. I was being prepared for something *more*. At the time, I wasn't sure what that was because I am on a faith walk. I live my life by Hebrews 11:1, or what I call, "Flying Blind but Trusting My Wings." My situation had given Grief a false sense of security. His overconfidence would be his demise.

As my confidence grew, Grief began to falter. When God takes over, it's over. You'd better be on the right side of the battle (which for years I felt like I wasn't). In all actuality, I was being set free from the bind of self-defeat. I slowly pulled away from Grief's hold on me and started leading. Spiritual muscle grows in the Processing Plant. So he was no match for me. I wasn't an abusive dance leader, as grief was, I showed mercy. He submitted willingly because I was ready for him too. As gospel artist Kathy Taylor's song so accurately states, "I've Got a Treasure from the Lord."

So that's my hustle and flow's dance with grief, and my prayer is that you, the reader, are encouraged by my dance, too.

Chapter 12

The Hustle and Flow of Kimberly Wiggins:
Tonight's Top Story

I hadn't seen my sweet friend in a few weeks. Rasheed and I had always wanted to attend her Zumba class. If you add her husband, we'd call it a double-date with weights. The guys always had a good time, sharing jabs regarding our rival college basketball teams. Rasheed and I met while we were undergraduate students at Duke University; our friends both attended the University of North Carolina. Somehow it worked. I truly enjoyed this lovely lady's positive spirit. However, our double date could never be rescheduled. My other half could never make good on that promise. He died about a year before this particular weekend, but it was time for me to attend for both of us.

I enjoyed every second of my friend's heart-racing class. It felt so good to move. My body was stiff. Most of my moves felt awkward as my limbs attempted high kicks and booty shakes, however, I started to feel the rhythm of life waft over me. I exhaled a bit of the grief that circled my heart and brain that day. I inhaled happiness. The exchange was priceless.

After class, we headed to an adorable chocolate shop. Forget salad and smoothies; this girl understood I needed something heavier as we caught up. The thick gelato calmed my emotions. She then asked the question I haven't been able to get out of my head for months: "Are you able to experience joy at all right now?"

I took a deep breath and shared my truth. I told her that I was focused on trying to find a way to live. I shared how the projects and adventures I'd undertaken in the last year had been welcome distractions. I was learning how to smile again.

But that question.

"I'm able to experience some happiness," I said as I dipped my spoon into the sweet scoop of strawberry cheesecake that was about to melt.

"I'm able to laugh at a joke and have some good moments, but joy. I haven't found joy yet. I've heard from others walking this path that it's possible. I'm starting to believe that's true, but my heart isn't there yet."

She let out a quick sigh.

I knew she understood.

She had been one of the first friends from my sorority that I called hours after *it* happened. I needed her to know my world had ended and to be ready to help me pick up the pieces.

You see, Rasheed had left our Orlando apartment on the evening of April 16th to pick up some stupid snacks. He never returned home. In the blink of an eye, my world changed in ways I never imagined possible. Three cars ran over him. State Highway Patrol troopers in Florida are still searching for the first two drivers.

But let's go back.

Back to the Beginning

I met Rasheed in September of 1998. I was a freshman: a sweet, naive, 17-year old. He was a handsome, sweet-talking, senior with all the moves. We shared only a few glances during that first year. Somehow, I always felt something more in those glances. Those few seconds our eyes connected as I hurried across the Quad to grab my chicken sandwich and Snapple on my way to Chemistry.

Years passed. Exams, parties, pizza, basketball games and fraternity and sorority parties were written into my story. I later graduated and entered adulthood. My unique childhood started to play a major role. Born in Houston, my parents moved the family to the Saudi Arabia when I was four years old. My dad's job transferred him. Everything changed. It wasn't just the food we ate, the roads we traveled, or even the fact my mom could no longer drive; that move opened my eyes to opportunities. I learned languages and made new friends. However, I always yearned for the end of the trips when we flew to

America. Home would remain the land of steak, bluebonnets, and big hair; I'm a proud Texan.

Americans aren't allowed to attend high school in Saudi Arabia so years later when I was about to enter high school, my parents moved to a suburb outside of Dallas. I became one of a handful of black faces in the hallways. I participated in numerous programs and clubs, but I also established one that my peers badly needed. My friends and I formed a panel that addressed the issue of race. I shared my personal brushes with racism. After each talk, at least one student would tell us if he or she had ever thought that words or actions, like the ones we referenced during our presentation, could negatively affect someone. It was then that I learned the power of communication and the power of having the right platform. I now realize those years discussing the world laid the groundwork for my career and for my life (i.e., what it's like to need a male driver to go to the grocery store or how I felt after being called a nigger while buying ice cream in a mall that broadcasted the Islamic call to prayer on the loudspeakers).

Years later, I worked, sweated, and earned two degrees. I knew I wanted to spend my life telling stories, but getting my foot in the door would prove more difficult than I imagined. I gained invaluable experience during several internships. After graduate school, I became an associate producer at a station in Miami. I went on to work at several other television news stations, and through it all, Rasheed was there. When viewers posted comments saying hurtful things, he comforted me and reminded me to focus on being the best journalist possible. When I was forced to cancel our dates or weekend trips for the opportunity to anchor or because I had landed a big interview, he always understood. Rasheed even spent a New Year's Eve with me in the studio in Cincinnati because I had been drafted to anchor a news special, and he always did it with a smile.

Building Upon That Foundation

I desperately wish I could go back in time to those moments when he physically supported me. To the days when we texted stupid things to one another throughout the day. To the days when I yelled at him for staying in the gym too long. To the days when he, I and our rescue puppy, Lola, spent all day inside on a Saturday eating pizza for all our meals because we were too lazy to go to the grocery store.

I'll even take most of April 16, 2016. It started off simply, sweetly and normally enough. A lazy morning in bed, pancake breakfast at the clubhouse, and then an afternoon at the movies. All while in sweats and a messy bun because that's when he swore I looked most beautiful.

I'm starting to see that time doesn't heal all wounds, but I read somewhere that it does "give you the tools to deal with all of them." You see, nearly two years out, the pain is still just as real as it was on April 17, 2016. In many ways- worse. I now know what it's like to live without *him*. That thing we both feared. The reason he asked me to stop knocking on criminals' doors to get their sides of the stories. The reason we moved closer to his job so he wouldn't have to drive an hour to work in heavy traffic.

But it got us anyway.

He worked so hard to protect me; to make sure I felt safe and loved. I tried my best to help him think three steps ahead and include the unfortunate "could be" scenario in possible plans. If only I had succeeded that night. That stupid night when he wanted some snacks and had them in his hands. He was feet away from our home-- from my arms, from our life.

Since the night Rasheed was killed, our families have truly been my rocks. I've been blessed with a great network of support. My friends have thought of things my brain couldn't. Strangers have even become friends by shining light on my darkest days. I know everyone doesn't have that luxury when the unthinkable happens, and I'm truly sorry for that reality. It's taken a village to help me survive major milestones. For example, Easter 2017 was his first "Angel-versary." However, we couldn't celebrate together. He couldn't suggest we throw some clothes in a bag and hop in the car so he could take me to that adorable bed and breakfast we loved in St. Augustine. I couldn't watch his eyes shine brightly as he took his first bite of a dessert I had made just for him. This one we each had to mark on our own. I lived through something I never thought was possible: living *our lives* alone.

Alone.

If I'm honest, I slowly remember what it was like to be on my own. We lived in different cities and towns for *seven years*. It strengthened our bond and taught us to communicate. I wish we had been able to spend those years together, but in a way, that time is helping me now. The muscle memory of knowing Rasheed was always in my corner – even though he couldn't often physically be in my corner is coming back to me.

Learning how to go long stretches without hearing that big, beautiful laugh. I've learned that the dead do talk back. We simply must listen closer. Certain breezes on clear days; the cardinal with its bold, red chest perched high on a nearby tree branch; the song with a message that pierces your heart at just the moment you needed – they all help me "hear" him. Though it's nowhere near those great hugs he gave me when he returned home from work, I still feel his presence surrounding me, but let's be honest, it's not the same.

I still remember the intense pain that filled me that first week. That ringing sound you hear in movies during the most difficult scenes. All I could do those first few days was curl into a ball. I mean literally, everything physically hurt. My heart throbbed. My heart still pains for his presence physically, but I'm trying. I'm hustling – *hard*, y'all.

I try to get up and push through each day to do what I think God has left me here to do.

Hustling Hard

We always tried to stay focused on the possibility of what could be, so that's my reason for living now: staying pressed toward my goals, our goals. I can still hear him cheering me on, beaming with pride. I can sometimes feel him pushing me out of bed, trying to stick the toothbrush in my hand to get me on my way on so many difficult mornings.

In many ways, I'm a shell of my old self. The sadness lives here -- sipping tea and eating butter cookies with the rest of my emotions. However, I've also grown into something I'm proud of, and I know he is, too.

My hustle to make things happen, to push myself to dream again and the flow of the love and energy we shared is manifesting itself in miraculous ways.

In the months after Rasheed's passing, I traveled to India, and I started writing again. I began working on legislation to prevent hit and run drivers from leaving the scene and escaping punishment; I helped launch scholarships in Rasheed's name; I bought our first home; I even planted the seed of an entrepreneurial endeavor and am watering and nurturing it.

95

A few months into my widowhood journey, I found a *wister* (widow sister) on Twitter. Roni Hollis blogged about the loss of her dear husband, Mike, and used the phrase "Still His" in her posts. It was also the name of her blog. We began liking each other's tweets. She even sent me some encouragement from her home across the country. One day it hit me: if that phrase brought me encouragement and joy, what if it could do the same for others in the same position? I messaged her and asked if she'd like to collaborate with the goal of encouraging others who are missing their mates. We had no idea what we were doing, and in many ways, we are still trying to figure it out. However, that phrase keeps us going – as do the stories we hear along the way.

Sharing the phrase "Still His" is to comfort those who know a void that can never be filled. It shows our connection to our loved ones and to our Lord. It's to help those who long for love from a spouse who can no longer hug you, kiss you, hold you and support you from within the rudimentary confines of this world, and during this tragedy, I choose to take another stand. I choose to celebrate the thing that makes me human, the thing that makes me want to live: love.

I will own the great love my man shared with me.

About nine months into my widow journey, we officially launched "Still His" – a company whose sole purpose is to encourage widows and provide hope and light along a path seemingly devoid of both.

When God Moves You

As I worked to figure out ways to spread the word about Still His, an old friend offered me a television interview on her local, talk show that broadcasted on the Eastern Shore. I happily made the drive, cried through the interview, and started to leave thinking that was it. However, God had another plan. As I made my way through the hall that once gave me so much joy when I showed Rasheed where his 'then-girlfriend' was learning how to live her dream of being a television journalist, my old boss stopped me. He shared condolences and then offered an opportunity that would help bring me back to life: a job as a morning anchor.

When Rasheed was killed, I had been out of the business for about a year and a half. As much as I enjoyed having time off from a full-time job, I knew I couldn't live like that forever. I had dreams and goals for myself that were starting to re-emerge. I said "yes" and moved to the Eastern Shore a few weeks later. The tranquility and access to nature are exactly what my soul needs right now. It is a bit softer and quieter here than working in some of the larger markets I've worked in, but I love it and know God led my heels here for a reason. I need a place where I can repair my heart and learn how to live with the gaping wound that might never fully heal. Though we may be able to smile brighter and laugh louder on some days, the heartache will always remain. In many ways, that's what this life is all about; learning to live with the loss.

Faith It

Weekends are often minefields of emotion. While your coupled friends enjoy precious time together, your new widowed reality means two days of quiet time that can be beyond difficult. Could it be because of its connection to faith? I now have a new appreciation for a reality I never gave much weight to when my heavenly angel was my earthly one. Recently, I had a real conversation with a beautiful friend. She reminded me "God is good. It's man that is terrible."

No, God doesn't want anyone of us to be raped, robbed, sick or killed. God hoped to provide a beautiful life for each of us to live in a beautiful world. However, when sin slithered into the equation, it changed everything. Free will entered the picture, and when a coward's free will rammed into my angel's simple errand, it ended in pain beyond measure.

My head also knows God can stop or change any situation.

That part -- the idea that Rasheed's death could have been stopped or changed or postponed or just happened a different way – one not so gruesome – tears apart my soul. However, within these last few months, I've begun to understand that my pain and suffering isn't the exception. Because of free will, pain is a part of all our stories. No one is immune. While God didn't promise us a life without hardships, He did promise to stand with us. While I wish I didn't have to fight this hardship without my man, I do know that doors that have been opened, the miracles I've already experienced, and the love I still feel around me on the days I can allow myself to feel it prove God is with us.

Returning to church took real work, prayer and time. My first time stepping foot into a church occurred eight months after Rasheed's funeral for the New Year's Eve Watchnight service at a church near Washington, D.C. we often attended while we dated. I attended with good friends – in fact, they're the couple whose wedding brought us together. It was difficult. I felt out of place and even worse because I felt that way. The hymns triggered memories of sitting in the same church years prior with my man. I was glad I attended, but it wasn't easy. Hours later, I boarded a plane and flew to Georgia to visit Rasheed's grave. A New Year's date with my love that no one could have ever predicted in 2015.

Living through a tragedy, such as grief, means you must learn to be easy on yourself. I enjoy more spa days than I should. I certainly eat more cake than my dresses like, but, sometimes, those little moments of joy are what get me through a day, a week, a month. I also proudly hold the right to live my truth – even if that includes learning to enjoy life as an independent woman who never remarries because she still feels married to the man she met when she was 17 years old. Does that mean that I don't miss flowers because it's Tuesday or the comforting feel of his hand on my lower back as he proudly walked into a room with me by his side? Of course not.

Living this life is difficult. The world sees what it wants. My heart feels the only thing it can, and nothing adds up to anything helpful. As a widow mentor told me, over time, the edges soften. The hardest part is knowing I must wait my entire lifetime to see him. The pain is there, but I'm able to live in the love he gave me every day of our time together and smile because of it. He will always be my husband. We had a relationship that those together ten times as long, aren't guaranteed to be blessed to experience. We have a love that soothes my soul. I will always try to remember to be glad that it happened. I pledge not to "move on," but to move forward, and my *wisters*; I urge you to do the same.

Chapter 13

The Hustle and Flow of Sabra Robinson: An Angry Black Widow

[Excerpts of this post were originally written for Hope for Widows Foundation and later included on the Black Women Widows Empowered website. This post has since been expanded for this book. I'm sitting here in tears and filled with bitter emotions as I relive my anger. I am human.]

I have a right to my anger, and I don't want anybody telling me I shouldn't be, that it's not nice to be and that something's wrong with me because I get angry. – Maxine Waters

Five years ago, I was married. Today, I am widowed. Herb, my husband of 23 years, passed away from cancer on February 24, 2012.

In April of 2011, he suddenly found himself with a bad stomach cramp, which turned into severe pain. I remember the day that I received a desperate call from him all too well.

Two Weeks' Notice

I was working for a cable broadcast company, and I had just given my two weeks' notice. Another offer came to me that I could not refuse. I had worked with the cable company for two years, and my pay had been cut. Our household was struggling. We both needed to work towards making more money. Then, out of the blue, a recruiter called me about a great opportunity, and well, I took it. Not a week into my two weeks' notice was when I received the call.

The Call

I was sitting at my desk trashing old documents and making way for my soon-to-be exit. My office phone rang with Herb's number on the caller ID. I thought nothing of it.

"Hey, what's up?" I answered.

"Sabe, I'm sick," he said with a moan.

I was concerned. Panic was in his voice. He never admitted to being sick.

"What do you mean?"

"I'm sick," he repeated.

My husband was sick, sick enough to go to Urgent Care. Shortly after he arrived, he called to tell me that they had referred him to the emergency room.

I left work to meet him. After we checked into the hospital and went through the required processes, we were given a room where they checked his vitals.

Blood pressure – √

Eyes – √

Nose – √

Throat – √

CT Scan – X

While his blood pressure, eyes, nose, and throat were fine, the CT scan showed a tumor behind his stomach.

DAMN!

It was downhill from there for nine months.

I was in and out of the office for those two weeks. They were kind and gracious and understood my plight, although they knew my final day on the job was near. In a way, it was refreshing because I was going to begin a new journey in a field I loved while having the ability to work from home. God worked out everything because He knew exactly what I needed.

The "Talk"

He needed a biopsy to tell us the nature of the mysterious mass. Herb had it during an outpatient surgery visit. We had the biopsy performed during an outpatient surgery visit. I was in the operating room, but I left due to my emotional distress. I didn't want him to see me.

After I waited a couple of hours, the doctor finally came in and took me to a private room. There, he told me Herb had Non-Hodgkins lymphoma.

I didn't know what say or do. I was alone. And I had to be the one to tell Herb on the drive home that he had cancer. I didn't want to and hadn't planned on telling him until the time was right.

But when would be the right time to tell someone you love that they have cancer?

That was the doctor's job!

As the medicine wore off, he slowly came around.

"What did they say?" he asked me.

I ignored him.

"What did they say?" he repeated.

Again, I ignored him.

"Come on. What did they say?"

I stuttered until it finally came out. "They said you have cancer."

"Cancer? What? Aww man." He was calm. He didn't scream or cry, but he was also still groggy from the surgery.

From there, our lives turned upside down.

Upon hearing the news, his mom immediately purchased a plane ticket and flew to Charlotte to live with us for seven months. She was a God-send.

I Hate the ER

After three months of aggressive chemo treatments, which ended a few weeks before Thanksgiving, most of his lymph nodes were gone except some in his neck.

All appeared to be good, right?

Wrong.

Two months later, at the end of January, he woke up with severe pain in his groin. Hearing him scream broke me. I had never heard this type of shriek before, and I never want to hear it again.

Since that night, we'd made several trips to the ER -- one in an ambulance -- and he didn't get better. The pain in his groin was from lymph nodes on his spine which impaired his ability to walk. Herb was prideful, and for several weeks, he limped on his own until his pride got the better of him and he used crutches.

We had several more hospital stays. When we called the oncologist and complained about the visits and severe pain, (his doctor was out of the country for two weeks, so we had to deal with his nurse), they finally ordered another MRI. Before that time, his last MRI showed nothing developing. Three weeks later, the next MRI showed lymph nodes.

After our MRI appointment, we returned home. Not even fifteen minutes later, we received a call. We needed to head to the hospital downtown, and it was a matter of life and death.

On our return, everything was prepared for us. Herb's temporary room was ready, and he was joking as usual. He said he was fine until the team of doctors took him to another room for his final head scan. His sister and I held his hand as we patiently waited in the hall. We had his mother on speakerphone.

Once the scan was done, we had to go to the thirteenth floor.

What's on the 13th floor?

The Intensive Care Unit.

I Hate the ICU

We finally made it to the ICU room, and they served him fried chicken, macaroni, and Jell-O. We shared the meal, laughed, and joked. His sister and I were happy. His first-born son called and spoke with him, and so did his parents and a few of his friends. He was in good spirits, and so was I.

Soon, things took a different turn.

He started vomiting and had an unbearable pain in his head. They allowed him to medicate himself through the touch of a button. Whenever the pain came, he'd press the thimble, and he would vomit. This continued in a vicious cycle.

Herb had an awesome male nurse who took care of him. He yelled over to him, "Do you know the Lord?"

"Yes, sir," the nurse respectfully replied.

Herb praised God during his pain. It was time for all visitors to leave, so I kissed him on his forehead and told him I would see him in the morning. He looked at me in a daze. All I could do was hope that he had heard me.

About an hour-and-a-half passed before Herb's sister called me in a panic. We had decided to take turns being with him so that one of us would always be with our daughters.

"Get to the hospital immediately," she said

I called my pastor's wife, and then I drove to my son's school to pick him up. When I arrived at the hospital, Herb was unconscious. His sister was crying hysterically and holding his hand. I must've been in shock -- I didn't know what to do or how to react. I called my older son, who lived an hour away, and told him to meet me at the hospital. My pastor, his wife, and my girlfriend, Rita, and my pastor's son, who was the Minister of Music at our church, came as well. We prayed. The doctor told us that he was in a coma, and the only thing keeping him alive was the ventilator, and I needed to make that dreaded decision of keeping him alive or allowing him transition on. I decided to allow him to leave because Herb never wanted to be kept alive on a ventilator.

Near 10:00 a.m. we received a sign of hope. He was snoring. His sister was thankful but, it wasn't snoring. The cancer had metastasized to his brain. There was no hope for survival.

His brain had begun to shut down.

As a last resort, the doctors performed several tests to see if he would react, but he failed them all. I took out my iPhone and played "Let it Rain" by Michael W. Smith in his ear. He didn't respond.

I had made the difficult decision to let him go. It was his wish.

The process took a few hours, and the wait was painful. It was the longest and most brutal wait I'd ever endured. When it was over, the room filled with prayer from my pastor and his wife. I am forever grateful for the leadership and praise team that came to support me in his room.

Then, the doctors informed us that it was time to say our goodbyes. It was a tough scene for me to witness. The last person to say goodbye was my oldest son. He cut off a piece of Herb's hospital robe to take with him, and we all left the hospital.

I Hated the Hustle

He was gone, and I was jobless. From the time he got sick to three weeks before his death, I was employed. I vividly remember the day when my boss sent me an instant message saying, "We need to talk."

Five minutes later, he told me the project I'd been working on had come to an end, and there was no need for me to continue. He thanked me for my services, and just like that, I was let go. I didn't see it coming, or maybe I should have. I was sidetracked by my husband's painful screams, his fainting while company visited, or his mother running to his side while I was on a conference call. You better believe I was sidetracked.

Although the contract ended earlier than expected, I still gave God all the glory. I had to. I grew up in the church, and it was there that I witnessed the operation of faith, praise, and song. I got to know God on a personal level, and naturally, my faith kicked in. And boy did it! But, I had to do the work, and work I did.

My money was low. I was unemployed, and I needed food. I looked around in my closet for something to sell and intentionally bypassed my Michael Kors purse, watch, and wallet. They still looked brand new because I had hardly used or worn them. After searching for other items, it was clear that I needed to give up something that I dearly loved. Besides, they were the only items that I knew I could sell without a problem.

I snatched up each item and set them aside while I placed an ad on Craigslist (this was in 2012, after all). Within fifteen minutes, I received a response. By the next day, I had received several e-mails and ended up settling up with two women.

It was around 9:00 p.m., and I received a call from one of the women who wanted to purchase the purse. My daughter was twelve at the time, so I brought her along. We met at a local Chick-Fil-A and exchanged my purse and wallet for $250.

Next Hustle

It was time for me to sell my watch. The customer worked from 9-5 through the day and the only time I could meet her was during her lunch. Thank God she worked close to my home. In fifteen minutes, I made $75 and had already received an e-mail thanking me for the watch.

It was a done deal.

I had food money!

From a sista who was too darn proud to (yet again) ask family for money, I had to do something this time. I put on my 'big girl pants,' and off I went to get humbled.

Another Hustle

I was still out of a job and had been submitting my résumé to employers on a daily basis. One position, in particular, caught my attention, and I went for it. Having a corporate background, I decided to do something different. I had to do what I needed to do to get employed, so I applied at Macy's for a part-time position selling retail. I got the job – as a Fashion Fair Cosmetics salesperson.

I couldn't believe it. They believed that I would be a good fit because of my prior experience as an Avon cosmetics representative. It didn't pay that much, but I was elated. By working in the cosmetics section, I found out the salary was a bit more than the average salesperson. And, I did something I liked to do – making people feel good about themselves.

After three months of hustling and ensuring I hit the sales goals, I got the call. I was offered a full-time corporate job making more money. The blessing was right on-time.

Mo' money!

Mo' money!

Mo' money!

I loved both jobs but knew I couldn't keep up the hustle of working for them both. God had seen me through some of the hardest moments in my life, and He blessed me back to monetary, emotional and spiritual normalcy.

It was all good for a while because the hustle began all over again -- from creating a GoFundMe account for my son's tuition to having my husband's car being hunted down from the bank because of his death (thank God the tow truck driver sympathized with me). The car note was in his name only, and because I didn't have Power of Attorney, I hit many obstacles. I could neither get ownership of his car nor could

I purchase another working vehicle.

The cycle had restarted.

Challenges kept coming.

My flow was immobilized.

I Hate Grief

I had to keep living through each and every challenge. That's who I was. I had to shrug off my wants and needs and put my children's needs first. That's what I had to do. I had to develop an action plan of getting my groove back. That's what I did.

I had to reinvent myself.

I ended up creating the Black Women Widows Empowered non-profit organization, a Facebook private support group, a widow's podcast, and this book project. I am humbled by the twelve women who chose to share their journey of grief and widowhood with the world. I'm excited about their next phases, and I can only imagine how hard it was for them to write their chapters. I thought I would be okay writing mine, but to be honest, I cried doing it.

But that's okay because healing starts with telling our story.

I still hate grief, but without it, I wouldn't be able to honor the experiences that come after a loss.

BONUS

A Widower's Journey Beyond the Horror: A Chat with Andre

It's not often you get to hear the widower's side of things, so I reached out to Andre Cox early in 2017 to obtain an unfamiliar sounding board. They grieve too, and Andre wanted to share his side of what he calls his 'horror' story.

Meet Andre Cox, a black widower from Teaneck, New Jersey.

***

BWWE: How long has it been since you became a widower?

Andre: Vikki died on March 28, 2014, so it will be three years soon.

BWWE: What has it been like since being a single dad? Tell us about your kids.

Andre: As a married man, I was so used to discussing things with Vikki concerning the kid; from dinner discussions, clothes to buy them, vacations to take, etc. When it came to the kids, decisions were predominately made together. I struggled at the beginning because when there was a decision to be made, I immediately thought to discuss it with Vikki only to discover she isn't there to provide her input. I am okay with knowing whatever I decide for them is for their best now. In the end, I did not sign up to be a single dad, but I am. It should be a mom and dad raising kids, but here I am raising them the best I can, and the kids are now 26, 20 and 12. At the time of her death, only the two youngest were living at home as they were 17 and nine years old while the oldest was 22.

My kids handled the death way better than I did. My oldest did struggle with it; he was the first born and knew her the longest. She had a special place for him, and he knew it. He has a creative spirit like she did and was willing to take chances in life to better his life. He enjoyed the fact that she went out of her way to make sure he had everything he wanted and he misses that connection. I am glad he can support himself and live on his own. I am proud of him being a young man trying to find his way and make a life. It's refreshing to be able to have adult conversations with him knowing those 20+ years ago; he was this innocent looking child. My middle child is a junior in college on a football scholarship. My late wife and I always said he is low maintenance out of the three kids. He was hurting because he saw how she changed physically and could not help her. He would pick her up and carry her around the house so she wouldn't have to walk. He brought her joy in his innocence and thoughtful ways. Although he seemed intent on injuring himself due to crazy stunts (she nicknamed him "Stuntman in Training"), he was just content to play outside. My daughter who is 12 handled it better than all of us. She and Vikki were inseparable. Vikki called her, "my shadow." She is such a happy, go-lucky child; always singing and loves to draw sing and has been playing the piano since she was six years old. She loves science, vowing to be a scientist who can draw when she grows up. She freely talks about her mom as if she is still here, referencing fond memories. She tells her older brother, "just because mom is not here don't mean you can break her rules." She is with me most of the time due to my son being away at college.

BWWE: What have you been doing to keep your mind off of your loss?

Andre: I struggled with handling it because after the house became quiet and the two were upstairs, I was left alone with just my thoughts. It hurt badly not to be able to do anything but think about her death.

Nearly a year after she died, I continued to blame myself because I felt I failed her. Husbands are supposed to take care of their wives and kids no matter what; I had to keep busy. My priority from the time she first was diagnosed with breast cancer was to make sure the kid's lives were not disrupted. Because I ran around with them before her sickness a lot, it wasn't difficult to keep it up. I just did not want them to be reminded, such as not being able to attend piano lessons because her mom has cancer, so I made sure she went. I made sure my son went to practice and his games because if not, he would think that it was because his mom has cancer. So because of my approach to making sure the kid's lives were not disrupted, I knew that I needed to make sure I was still around. I became more social by going out, attending family functions and meeting people. My family and friends helped a lot, checking in on me making sure I was okay.

Also, I took up bike riding more, which serves as a way to get back in shape plus it's therapeutic because I ride and think (good thoughts). Now that my daughter is getting older, I can get out more. Also, I always enjoyed cooking and am finding myself getting back into cooking. I have an upcoming trip to Mardi Gras in New Orleans coming up in February 2017.

BWWE: Over 30 years ago, the five stages of grief was developed by Elisabeth Kubler-Ross. They are Denial, anger, bargaining, depression, acceptance. How would you rate each one on a scale from 1-5, with five being the highest?

Andre:

5 – Depression

4 – Denial

3 - Anger

2 – Bargaining

1 - Acceptance

BWWE: As a black male widower, do you feel that you have experienced any unique challenges with your grief/mourning? How did you overcome them? Did you overcome them?

Andre: Vikki's passing was like a "horror show" except, unlike the movies, it was really happening. Dealing with her death, I have learned to live with it. I will never forget but always live with it. Sometimes we resist acknowledging we want to move on but that is how life is. We are born to die, and all of us will experience this.

I remember being happy in my life at times before she died, so I am open-minded about finding happiness again. I am opening my mind about what life has yet to show me. In the end, I do not see my experience and challenges differently than others; it just plain sucks! I questioned less of the "why." There isn't anything I can do anymore about *why*. I feel it will not prevent me from moving on because, in a way, I feel that I have moved on. Regardless of me thinking about it or being reminded in some way, I am living for me. Also, I learned that the more I tell someone the story, the easier it is to tell it, thus assisting me in moving on, living life. Because of her death, I joined bereavement groups and had many personal therapy sessions with a therapist. It helped me open up and was able to publicly acknowledge what was wrong with me due to her death. I needed to know it was okay to share with others how I feel. I think I shocked some members of the group because first off, I was the only male of 30+ women in the group and I eventually opened up in discussing it. I shocked myself.

I never felt I was suicidal; the thought never crossed my mind. Generally speaking, I do not think the overall experience as a black male cause any unique challenges. I do caution those who are married to have those difficult conversations about what to do if one dies like being prepared financially and if kids are involved, especially young kids, make sure you have a prepared plan in place to who will take care of them just in case both of you are gone. Having a will is a necessary evil and prevents making dealing with his or her death worse.

BWWE: In the book, *Widower: When Men Are left Alone* (a book that interviewed 20 bereaved men and provides results), it touches on how men mourn differently than women, are less expressive, and often very reticent. Can you identify with this statement?

Andre: As a male, in general, I feel men tend to keep things in so that we do not show we are losing it. Sometimes that 'testosterone macho crap' gets us in trouble. I tend to keep things in and not share it, but that is always how I have been. I have heard that widowers are likely to run out and find another woman to replace their spouse faster than women finding another man. I don't know how true that is. I am not running around trying to get married so fast. I feel I can find love again, but willing to take my time and naturally let it happen. I can remember a family member telling me that I will find love again and remarry. I was so angry with that person at the time. Over time I realized that because I am here, life must be lived and part of that is finding someone.

BWWE: Thank you, Andre, for your transparency about your journey onward after your wife's passing. All the best to you and the kids and I hope you find solace and fun on your Mardi Gras trip!

Notes

17   **the widow has the power to cause death**: Oke, Ruth, O. (2013). "Widowhood Practices Among the Yoruba and Igbo of Nigeria as a Form of Violence Against Women" in Rose Mary Amenga-Etego and Mercy Amba Oduyoye (Eds), *Religion and Gender-Based Violence – West African Experience*. p. 437-438.

17   **A lot of weight when you're well:** Bambara, Toni Cade, 1992. *The Salt Eaters*, New York: First Vintage Contemporary Press, p. 10.

Letters to the Authors

To Melody Dixon-Brown,

Wow! It's hard to believe how far we've come since dad's passing, and every step of the way you've been even stronger. More amazed that my mom is an author, and I'm not surprised! You have been working so hard focusing most of your time between school, family and your outside organizations. But you finally accomplished something you enjoy doing. Therefore, I'm very proud of you and hope you keep it up.

Your son,

Robert Brown

***

To LaTisha Bowie,

LaTisha, I'm extremely happy for you and excited about your contribution. I admire your strength, courage, resilience, and brilliance. Keep being unstoppable my beautiful sister.

Tamlyn Franklin, HowToBecomeAnUnstoppableBlackWoman.com

***

To Rhonda Butler,

While we didn't know that this would be a journey that we would be walking together ("Follow Me"), I know that GOD has a purpose for everything. I am proud of you for sharing this part of your life and being a support to others around you. Continue to walk in your purpose. GOD loves you, and so do I!

Adrienne Lindsey

***

To Angela Allen,

Angela, I'm so excited and proud of you for taking part in the writing of this book. Truly you are an Inspiration to me as well as others. Thank you for sharing your heart with myself and others. Remember as you always say, Iron sharpens Iron.

Danyell Shaw, Minister- www.widowsvoice.webs.com

To Cheryl Barnes,

Your love for Tony shines through. Through your words, we are all blessed to know him and be witness to love that you shared. I know he is smiling down on you with pride, and eternal love.

John Polo, Author & Speaker

www.betternotbitterwidower.com

***

My Dearest Kerry,

Without you, so many of us young widows would have been left unvalidated in our grief. You have given so many of us a non-judgmental, open, and humorous place to fall, with the sharing of yourself and your stories.

Thank you so very much,

Michelle Miller

***

To Beverly Kelley Jeter,

I thank you from the bottom of my heart for extending your story to this book collaboration. You helped me as my partner in compiling and reviewing the stories, and now you are an author! Thank you for your love, positivity, and light. Shine on my sista!

Sabra Robinson

***

To Beverly Kelley Jeter,

You have blessed me enormously. Please receive my deepest gratitude for the continued love, kindness and support on behalf of the Rona widows and orphans whom you have only met through me. Thank you for believing in me.

Roseline Orwa

www.ronafoundation.co.ke

***

To Beverly Wallace,

You are such a gem, and I appreciate you as a woman of faith. I'm so glad our paths have crossed. Your story truly inspired me. Thank you for your unconditional friendship and support. Love you!

Sabra Robinson

***

To Kimberly Holmes-Wiggins,

Thank you for inspiring me every day and for being the best 'wister' and business partner I could ask for! You are beautiful, kind, and full of grace. I know that is why Rasheed loved you and still loves you so!!

Roni Hollis

Author and Entrepreneur

www.StillHis.com

***

To Danielle James,

I'm so proud to be your sister, and even more proud of what you've done with this book. This is your season, Sissy! God's not done with you yet.

Karen Paige, Paparazzi Consultant

www.KarenPaige.com

***

To Maureen and Khadija,

I admire you both for having the discipline and energy necessary to frame and finish your writing project. Opening your heart once again to write about your grief journey takes a lot of courage. Your husband does matter and always will. He is part of you and who you've become and what you are to be. To share that life is precious and fragile, that grief is always there; sometimes it drives us, other times it breaks us is inspiring. This project will impact your audience and I am happy to know and support you both. Congratulations on your fantastic achievement! I am so proud of you ladies!

Chasity Williams, Co-Director

www.HopeForWidows.org

Questions and Topics for Discussion

1. In Chapter 1, A Black Widow's Journey Towards Living Life Anew, Wallace mentions several seasons of "hurricanes". Which of her seasons do you most identify with and why? Have you found love after the death of your husband only for him to die, too? If so, discuss how his death has impacted you.

2. In Chapter 2, The Life of the Paparazzi Party, can you identify with Danielle's dating hustle? If yes, how? Danielle struggled with keeping a relationship because of her PTSD and being open and honest with her dates. Have you struggled with an illness or disease and neglected to tell your mate?

3. In Chapter 3, Caterpillar, Cocoon, Butterfly, Evolution, LaTisha speaks about how her vision board activity a few years after her husband died. She admitted that she lost her identify along the way and struggled with the activity. Have you tried this activity before post loss of your husband? If so, was it hard for you to participate? LaTisha also discusses how her husband took his life. Can you relate to LaTisha's husband's death? If not, discuss how your husband's death has made an impact on you emotionally, physically, spiritually and mentally. If you can relate, discuss how his suicide has made an impact on you and what steps you have taken, or would like to take, to begin or continue the healing process.

4. In Chapter 4, A Black Woman's State of Mental Health, Khadija admittedly discusses her bout with mental illness. She took the necessary steps and sought out grief counselors. Has this chapter resonated with you at any point? If so, how? If not, discuss your feelings about seeking professional help. Would you consider seeking help? She also discusses religion and grief. Was your faith community supportive during your mourning?

5. In Chapter 5, Rebuilding Me After His Hustle Ended, Cheryl and her husband had prior discussions about what to do if either one of them had to be placed on a respirator at the End of Life. They decided that it would be for the best not to continue life. Cheryl made the decision, and his life ended. Have you ever been placed in this difficult situation?

6. In Chapter 6, Broken Crayons Still Color, Kerry discusses how she had learned of her husband's death after church while sitting in the church parking lot. Her happiness soon turned to dread after an

exciting worship service. Have you ever been put in a situation like this of one moment being happy and joyful and the next moment your joy turns to grief? Do you consider yourself a broken crayon capable of coloring?

7. In Chapter 7, A Pastor's Wife's Bitterness of Black Tea, Rhonda shares her story of faith, hope, joy, and growth in the church. Her husband was a minister who soon realized he could no longer minister due to his health. Has your husband ever decided to discontinue an activity because of his health?

8. In Chapter 8, The Drink that Remains, Beverly states, "…throwing that drink away would be like throwing away a part of him." She did not throw away the last drink that he shared with her at their home until weeks later. Have you held on to anything that reminded you of him? She also shares her need to enjoy life and go out on dates and eventually had a five-year relationship. She also shared that he was the first man to tell her that he loved her. If you have started dating, has your mate implied the same statement? If so, how did hearing those words make you feel?

9. In Chapter 9, My Destiny into Dating Continues, Angela reveals that she never expected to be called a widow at a young age because she viewed the term as antiquated. How did you feel when you first realized that you were now a "widow"? Not long after the death of her husband, she was asked if she would ever remarry again. Have you ever been asked this question so soon after his death? She also states that she received her very first wedding invitation after his death. Discuss how attending weddings may or may not trigger a 'grief alarm' (a trigger that brings back a memory of something).

10. In Chapter 10, Journaling My Despair of Mental Health and Self-Therapy, Melody finds her healing through journaling. Has journaling comforted you in your time of grief? Would you consider journaling if you haven't already?

11. In Chapter 11, My Dance with Grief, Maureen identifies her pain through songs and imagines dancing with Grief itself, which is truly an imaginative concept. Read her chapter aloud and imagine yourself dancing with grief. Interact with one another and show how you would dance with Grief.

12. In Chapter 12, Tonight's Top Story, Kimberly's chapter discusses a variety of events: growing up in another country as a black girl, racism, becoming a journalist, long-distance dating, and how her

husband went out for snacks and never came back. Discuss any of these events and how you overcame them.

13. In Chapter 13, An Angry Black Widow, Sabra provides a glimpse into her world of her husband's death. She opens up with Congresswoman Maxine Waters' quote: *I have a right to my anger, and I don't want anybody telling me I should be, that it's not nice to be and that something's wrong with me because I get angry.* Do you consider yourself an angry black widow?

Author Bios

Dr. Beverly Wallace is currently the Assistant Professor of Pastoral Care and Counseling at Shaw University Divinity School. She is an ordained Lutheran Pastor and was formerly the Assistant to the Bishop for the Southeastern Synod of the Evangelical Lutheran Church in America. In her capacity as Assistant to the Bishop, she was responsible for the candidacy for persons seeking rostered leadership in the ELCA and also served as the Coordinator of Pastoral Care for the Katrina Recovery Effort on the coast of Mississippi working with congregations (pastors and their members) and relief volunteers in the needed work after that disaster. After 9/11, Dr. Wallace was also involved in the Ambiguous Loss Project caring for persons in New York and is currently working on a research project to look at the impact of Hurricane Matthew on African Americans in rural areas in North Carolina.

Danielle James grew up in Alabama. She became a widow at the age of 32. She was married for only five short years to her late husband, Marcus James Sr. She is the mother of their two beautiful and intelligent children, Marcus James Jr. and Gia James. Danielle James received an Associate of Science Degree from Bishop State Community College in 2003. She obtained a Bachelor of Arts Degree in Anthropology from the University of South Alabama in 2005. She worked as a case manager for Alta Pointe Health Systems for nine years before the unfortunate loss of her husband on June 2nd, 2013. Danielle left Alta Pointe in September of 2013 and was on a journey to comprehend her new life. Danielle spends her free time reading, spending time with family and friends and participating in fitness activities to help strengthen her mind, body, and spirit. She continues to move up in her Paparazzi businesses as she is now a Premier Director, Crown 10 Member, and a member of the Life of the Party Bronze Access Program. She wants to use this platform to start a nonprofit for young black widows with children. You may visit her website at www.ChicJewelsAndAccessories.com

LaTisha M. Bowie was tragically inducted into the widow club on the morning of March 18, 2011, at the tender age of 31. It was on this day that her husband and companion of 17 years chose to end his life and completed suicide. As she navigated through the complicated grief process with two young children, LaTisha found that support and resources in this area of loss were minimal or lacking. This sparked LaTisha to become an advocate for families and individuals processing through the trauma of suicide; which culminated in the creation of Dialogos: Survivors Support and Postvention. Dialogos is a non-profit organization that offers scholarships and healing support through face to face and online support groups to individuals and families struggling with the after-effects of loss due to suicide. Dialogos also advocates for survivor awareness, and the elimination of the shame, blame, and guilt, that survivors often face after the loss of a loved one. Professionally, LaTisha is an educator, teaching students with Emotional Impairments and Mental Health disorders by day; and teaching future teachers as an Adjunct Professor of Special Education at the University of Michigan by night. She is currently completing her Doctorate in Special Education/Curriculum and Instruction. You may visit her Facebook page at www.Facebook.com/Dialogos-Survivors-Postvention-Support

Khadija Ali is a coach, motivational speaker, and author. Her passion for helping women evolve and transform their lives stems from triumphing over the tragedy in her own life. In 2007, she found herself a single mom to five children after losing her husband to colon cancer. Overnight, she had to figure out how to settle her husband's estate and find housing for her and her five children. It was a wake-up call for this newly widowed woman! In 2012, Khadija asked ten other young widows to write a book about their experiences. Only two widows, Maureen Bobo and Chasity Williams, continued with the book, "The Unwelcome Committee". The book is not only significant to losing a spouse but to comprehend and grasp the outlook of grief overall. When Khadija is not coaching, speaking, or writing, she hosts 'Evolutionary Woman Radio' on Blog Talk Mondays and Thursdays 5:30 pm. You may visit her page at www.HopeforWidows.org

Cheryl Barnes was born in Atlanta, Georgia. She attended college at Indiana University Bloomington, majoring in Public and Environmental Affairs Management. While she attended college, she met Martin "Tony" Barnes. They became inseparable and were married December 24, 1991. After five years of marriage, their first son, Malcolm, was born on New Year's Eve, 1991. After Tony obtained his Master's Degree in Social Work, the family moved to Orlando, Florida where she was employed by her dream job, Walt Disney World. Two years later, their second son was born. Cheryl later left Disney and accepted a job in accounting with a property management company. After the death of her husband in 2014, and as a way to work through her grief, she started writing, at first, only for herself. But, being encouraged by others, she began publishing her blog, "Widowness and Light." She is also a guest blogger and board member for blackwomenwidowsempowered.com. You may visit her page at www.ThinkAboutTellingsMyStory.Wordpress.com

Kerry Phillips is determined not to allow grief to drag her under. Kerry chose to become an advocate for the widowed community, sharing her own journey and those of other young widows. Realizing there was a void for widows and widowers wanting to venture back into the world of dating, she started Young, Widowed & Dating online support group providing a safe, supportive and nonjudgmental forum for the widowed community to share their dating adventures—hits and misses.

Her weekly blog - of the same name - covers topics ranging from relationships with in-laws to dating while raising children and everything in between. Kerry is also a blogger for The Huff Post, covering loss and grieving, Hope for Widows Foundation and covHERstories, a lifestyle blog. She is currently Vice President of a strategic marketing and communications company specializing in luxury senior housing. Additionally, she writes and ghostwrites for publications catering to older adults and seniors. You may visit her page at www.YoungWidowedandDating.com

Rhonda Butler is a native of Central Missouri residing in Columbia, MO; a widowed Pastor's wife who served alongside ministry of her husband-pastor Rev. William Butler, Jr. since 1978; mother of four children – David, Andrew, Christopher & LaShawn, and grandmother of eight (known as 'momma Butler to many); and she serves as member of local & state Missionary Baptist Minister Wives & Widows Auxiliary. Over the years, Rhonda has had the opportunity to share as a facilitator for various ministry groups. She's currently serving a second term as president of the Mt. Carmel Missionary Baptist District Association and as editor of the Missionary Baptist State Convention of Missouri Minister Wives/Widow auxiliary. Additionally, she is proudly approaching 30 years of service at the University of Missouri-Columbia where she has worked in Admissions Minority Recruitment, School of Social Work and currently as the Administrative Assistant to the Director of Residential Life (Housing).

Beverly Kelley Jeter became a widow in March 2010 after being married for almost 25 years. Her late husband, Chase, had been sick and hospitalized but was expected to return to work on the following Monday. He died the Thursday before from complications due to Sarcoidosis. Beverly and her sons struggled but managed through the days and continued to do so with help from family, friends, therapy and online grief support. Beverly graduated from

Douglass College, part of Rutgers University with a liberal arts degree. Beverly worked for a local government agency for over 33 years but decided to retire in April 2012 after her brother was murdered. She is currently working part-time as an aid for a young woman. In her free time, Beverly has volunteered as a *baby cuddler*, Moms Demand Action for Gun Sense in America, participated in the Million Woman March of 2017 and campaigned for the Democratic party.

Angela Richardson Allen was born in Lynwood, California and she attended the Los Angeles public school system where she excelled in her studies. She went on to obtain a B.A. degree in Graphic Arts from San Diego State University and then an M.B.A. from National University. Also, she is a member of Zeta Phi Beta Sorority. Angela Richardson Allen is motivated by helping and serving others. She has always had a passion for helping those in need, particularly young women, and children. This passion led her to start a nonprofit organization, Total Renaissance Woman which was dedicated to helping at-risk youth, women in Crisis and teaching life skills. Her compassion to serve has led to her involvement in several ministries including, Possum Talks Prison Ministry, Dallas Juvenile Detention Center and Human Trafficking Initiatives. Angela is the President and Founder of Masterful Collective, a Sports and Event Marketing Boutique Firm and The Allen Insurance Agency. Angela has worked with Professional Athletes, Off the Field Player's Wives Organization and several organizations raising much-needed funds for these charitable organizations. Angela has always had a passion for entrepreneurialism even as a child, which she recalls having a lemonade stand in her neighborhood as an adolescent. Angela is a licensed Missionary and a devout Christian. Additionally, along with her daughter Amaya, they co-authored a book titled A Far Away Place geared to help children cope with death and grief.

Melody Dixon-Brown is a senior lecturer in the Department of Communication Studies. Lecturing at UNC Charlotte since 1999, Melody is a faculty advisor and lecturer on business communication, event planning, and small group communication. She brings almost 20 years of corporate experience that included BBDO Advertising and DuPont. Her published work includes "Shared Teaching: Models for Business Communications in a Research Environment," Business Communication Quarterly. Also, Melody co-presented, "Business Presentations: Providing Teaching Guidelines & Feedback to Students" at the 2005 Southeast Regional Conference of the Association for Business Communication in Greensboro, NC. She has a dual

128

degree in marketing and communications management from Syracuse University and an MBA from The University of Delaware.

Maureen Bobo is a Christ follower, Love Advocate, Speaker, Author, Social Worker, and Mom-preneur. Her ministries include grief, singles, and health and wellness. Maureen is a single parent of two daughters ages fourteen and seven. She became a single parent on April 7, 2010, when her husband of thirteen years, Martin Quinn Bobo, passed away of chronic heart disease at the age of forty-five. The children at that time were ages eight years and two months old. The grief from that tragedy led Maureen to develop The Beautiful Stones Ministries, in which the goal is to provide love and support to the grieving heart through grief support groups and social services. Maureen is a CoDirector at Hope for Widows Foundation, an organization that supports widows through the grieving process and beyond by providing life transition resources and immediate peer connections; facilitating the healing process and allowing them to rebuild and re-engage in life. Maureen is a co-author of 'The Unwelcome Committee'; the story of three young widows with children and their navigation through the processes of grief and also a contributor to the Grief Diaries book series, "Poetry & Prose and More," a heartfelt collection of expressive writing by 18 women as they journey through different struggles including loss, mental illness, and more. You can visit her page at www.HopeforWidows.org

Kimberly Holmes Wiggins joined the tender club of widowhood in 2016. She lost her soulmate at the age of 35 in 2016. Kimberly met Rasheed at Duke University. He was a senior, and she was a freshman. The two dated for seven years (all long distance) and were married for nearly five years. They were equally yoked and truly bound together by God, however, that physical bond was broken in April 2016. That's when Kimberly's beloved husband walked to the store to grab some snacks and never returned home. He was taken from her in a horrific hit and run incident. Police are still searching for two of the three drivers. She's doing everything in her power to aid that search. Professionally, Kimberly has a wealth of journalism experience. From reporting and anchoring to shooting, editing and producing, she's done it all, and sometimes, all in the same day! She's currently a morning anchor at WBOC-TV on the Eastern Shore of Maryland, Delaware, and Virginia. Prior to that position, she was responsible for covering health and education stories for the special projects department at WOFL-TV in Orlando. She also had general assignment reporting duties and helped manage the special projects department. Lastly, she often filled-in on the anchor desk for every newscast--- usually at a moment's notice. Her heartfelt coverage of an officer's funeral earned her an award from the Associated Press. Before landing in Central Florida, she was the weekend anchor & special projects reporter at WXIX-TV in Cincinnati and WBOC-TV in Salisbury, Md. Her career began behind the scenes as an associate producer in Miami and as a field producer at Bloomberg TV in their Washington, D.C. bureau. She has also launched a faith-based, retail company with a *wister* (widow sister) called Still His for those who would like to share their love for the Lord and/or for a spouse (whether here on Earth or up above)! They recently formed a partnership with the popular group, The Dinner Party, to launch support-based gatherings that are full of good food, laughter, and understanding for widows navigating the waters of significant loss and grief. Kimberly graduated from Duke University and Columbia University's Graduate School of Journalism. You may visit her page at www.StillHis.com

Sabra Robinson: Baltimore native and Charlotte, North Carolina resident Sabra Robinson is the creator and founder of Black Women Widows Empowered (BWWE). She was married to the love of her life Herbert Robinson for 23 years. Their union produced Roderick, Kolin, Bradley, and Terah. Sadly, Herbert succumbed to Non-Hodgkin's lymphoma in 2012. Seeking solace and support for her own grief, Sabra noticed the lack of organizations and informational groups that focused on the uniqueness of the Black woman's grief, loss, and mental health issues. Realizing that widows of color face bias, bigotry, prejudgment and intolerance, Sabra envisioned a safe, online and in-person nonprofit organization that identified with the unique circumstances and challenges that Black Women Widows encounter. A proud Morgan State University graduate, Sabra holds a General Theology Certificate from Oral Roberts University and studied at Gordon-Conwell Theological Seminary. Multitalented, yet humble, she facilitated a children's book and work-life Christian workplace conference(s) with former Survivor contestant and Christian radio personality Leslie Nease, Dr. Gail King, author, speaker and CEO of Handle Your Business Girl Empowerment Network and Allison Bottke, author of the *God Allows U-Turns* and *Setting Boundaries* book series. Sabra has also been sought after locally as well as abroad as a speaker and has also been recognized by the ABC Talent Development Program for her proposal to bring her children's book, *Micky, Ticky, Boo! Says Hello* to film. Sabra is even more excited to relay her new initiative, *Wounded, But Resilient Sistas Grief Support Group*, which is a monthly, face-to-face personalized support system for women to "read, relay, and recharge" from their grief and loss. Sabra also takes pleasure in focusing on her monthly grief podcast where she discusses various topics such as dating, grief, loss and awareness campaigns with widows and widowers of all backgrounds.

Volunteering with the Junior Achievement Foundation, ministering at Alzheimer's nursing homes, and leading life-group studies were a few examples of Sabra's commitment to volunteerism. However, the activities that bring her the most joy are going to the movies (she's a movie buff), encouraging others of their potential and laughing uncontrollably with her children. You may visit her pages at www.BlackWomenWidowsEmpowered.com or www.BlogTalkRadio.com/BlackWomenWidowsEmpowered

CPSIA information can be obtained
at www.ICGtesting.com
Printed in the USA
BVOW03s1503301217
503979BV00001B/79/P